Whatever's Next...

It's Not 13th Grade

A Dorm Mom's Guide For A Parent's Journey

Rebecca M. Adair

Copyright © 2020 by Rebecca M. Adair
Whatever's Next, It's Not 13th Grade! A Dorm Mom's Guide For A Parent's Journey

All rights reserved. No part of this publication may be reproduced, distributed, or transmitted in any form or by any means, including photocopying, recording, or other electronic or mechanical methods, without the prior written permission of the publisher, except in the case of brief quotations embodied in critical reviews and certain other noncommercial uses permitted by copyright law.

The resources in this book are provided for informational purposes only and shouldn't be used to replace the specialized training and professional judgment of a health care or mental health care professional.

ISBN: 978-1-7344737-0-4 (ebook)
ISBN: 978-1-7344737-1-1 (Paperback)

This book is dedicated to:

My heavenly Father—because none of this would be possible without His plan, His mercy, and His grace.

My own kids—the ones I brought into this world and get to experience it with—when we're all not too busy. Thank you for allowing me to share your stories.

My other kids—the ones I had the joy and privilege of advising, teaching, coaching, or mentoring. I learned much more from you than you did from me!

My husband—who helped "raise" **all** of them with me and has supported me in every way possible. Consider this large dragon officially slayed!

My friends—who may still think I'm crazy for my career path but are there for me anyway.

My colleagues—most of whom are still out there making a daily difference, while others have taken a well-deserved retirement!

My parents—who provided me with the best possible education, even if I didn't know it then.

Download the audiobook free!

READ THIS FIRST

Just to say thanks for buying my book, I'd like to give you the audiobook version 100% free!

To download and start listening, go to: http://bit.ly/2HvFIuF

Contents

Introduction..IX
How to use this book..1
How this book can help different groups....................5
Why should you listen to me?...............................39
2 kids, 2 paths...45
My professional experience.................................59
Ready or not?..85
Your background matters...................................105
How do you get help?......................................121
What's the parents' role?.................................147
What's the student's role?................................153
What if not college?......................................157
Rebecca's Recommended Resources...........................169
Acknowledgements..171
About the author..173

Introduction

First, I apologize to my residence life colleagues for using the word *dorm*. It made sense for this book, but I know it grates on you. Most people don't know that we say residence hall instead, and that a residence hall is a place that promotes community, not just a bunch of rooms.

This book started out in my mind as a "how to." The original "how to" focus was going to show parents how to avoid being the dreaded "helicopter parents." I could spend paragraphs explaining that term, but, in this case, it would be better to Google it! You'll find some definitions, articles, and cartoons. Some are funny and some are sad.

As I wrote it, this book morphed. It became a memoir of my time working at colleges and universities, and my time as a parent. But a memoir isn't usually written to help people. It's written to remember, entertain, or explore universal truth. While I enjoyed remembering and hope to entertain a bit, what I *most* want is to ease your way.

With this book, I want parents to learn from what I saw, what I did, and what I wish I'd done.

Many parents aren't prepared for having college-age students—whether those students attend college or not. I've also seen many students arrive at college unprepared—and frequently unwilling to be there—but that issue isn't within the scope of this book.

In my more frustrated moments, I see that a huge issue of the U.S. public school system is confused parenting and rapidly changing societal expectations. There's no way I can cover all that—much less say how to fix it. That won't stop me from doing what I can in an area where I feel I have some experience and expertise.

My focus in this book is the parents or supporters of students who are nearing graduation from high school. It's also for parents of students who are years away but *hoping* to attend college. And it's for those who are already in college and it's not going well. Those of you with much younger students might be able to look ahead and get some tips to prevent some of what gets students off track. I know, when they're just learning to read, it's tough to imagine them buying $200 textbooks!

In this book, I offer you an insider's look at higher education, a parent's dramatically different experience with two different children, and an academic coach's advice for how to be a successful (and sane) parent of a college student. **Or not.**

The "or not" doesn't apply to the sane part. It applies to the college part. Over the last few years of my career, I've discovered that many students **do not need to attend college**. And there's a variety of reasons for that.

Some aren't ready. Some aren't interested. Some aren't qualified. Some can be quite successful in a productive and healthy career *of their choice* without attending college. The most important thing for you to realize, as a parent or supporter, is that it's the **student's** choice. Period.

Because it's free, or because *you* went to college, or because it's the only way they can be a doctor and that's what you've always wanted for them—none of these are great reasons to attend, unless they're coupled with the student's willingness *and ability* to do what it takes to be successful. Not **your** willingness or ability. **Theirs.** If you want it for them more than they want it for themselves, that's the heart of the problem.

This book can show you how things work leading up to college, and how things work once your student is admitted. It will dispel some myths and let you in on some of the "secrets" known by professionals in the field.

If you have a student who is ready and willing, this book will show you how to be the kind of supporter who encourages *without* interfering. The kind of supporter who helps the college staff teach the student to fish, instead of catching, cleaning, cooking, and chewing the fish for them.

If you have a student who isn't ready and/or willing, this book can show you how to help them figure out the best path that **isn't** college. At least not yet (if ever). And that's okay! We'll talk about how to shift your expectations of what success looks like for your kids and better understand a positive role for yourself.

You'll read about my credentials and my experiences, but, for now, it might help to know that I have 30 years of experience working on a college campus. For 11 of those years, I *lived in the dorm,* surrounded by college students, day and night, as a full-time professional.

To some of you, it might matter that I have a master's degree in adult learning. (I define adults as those beyond high school, regardless of whether their behavior earns them that label.) I spent several years working on that degree while living with hundreds of college students, so I took away some lessons that can help you.

Finally, a factor that might matter more to some of you than to others, I'm a parent (and a stepparent). Of the four children who had me as a parent or stepparent, two have master's degrees, one has a bachelor's degree, and the fourth has a couple of free t-shirts from orientation.

I continue to learn from and with them, as well as from and with the students who used to "report" to me on campus. Many of them have become close friends, calling my husband and me their "college dad and mom," and backing that up with regular visits, wedding invitations, and calls about expecting children.

By reading this book, you can give yourself a chance to handle this tough age better than expected. Or maybe it's your second try, and you want to get it *right* this time. Or maybe you plan way ahead, and just know that when the time comes, you'll want to have taken some steps early on. Regardless of what stage your children are at, you can learn tips and strategies for being a successful supporter of a college-age student.

When I started writing this book, I contacted friends and colleagues who might have something to add. One of them, Kathy Harris, has a

13-year-old who is a remarkable young man. Both she and her husband are educated professionals. She asked how she could help (she's a writer) and I suggested she just "brain dump" a few questions she already has. What she sent me was somewhat of a surprise, as I happen to know this kid is doing great things already, making his parents proud on a regular basis. Here's what she sent me.

One of the things I worry about balancing as Mac gets well into high school is how much to push him and stay on top of his grades, etc. We do it now in hopes he'll figure out how to do this on his own for high school and college. But what if he doesn't? High school grades mean so much now for getting into college. And of course, his mental health always must come first—he's already stressed in middle school. I'm rambling...not expecting an answer but it's on my mind a lot—he's in 8th grade!

Kathy is an involved (but not hovering) parent, with solid education and the ability to communicate beyond what's normal. If these are **her** questions, I can only imagine what parents who have less experience and fewer resources are thinking. The good news is there are plenty of people on each campus who are qualified, ready, and eager to help!

Knowing how rapidly things change in our society—yet much stays the same—I want this book to give you tools that will change with the times. The idea is for you to be able to modify the tools to fit your situation for as many college-age kids as you plan to support!

It's critical to remember they're *individuals*. Even twins are separate individuals, as alert parents of multiples have reassured me. Learn how to figure out what your student needs, and what **you** need, to navigate this time well.

Readers usually want proof that what they're reading is true and/or useful. I can't argue with that! Sometimes, the best proof is in seeing what **not** to do. I have examples of that.

For those who want reassurance that their son or daughter will make it through college without a glitch or a mistake, you're on the wrong planet. Mistakes are the trademark of college students. For years, my job seemed to be making sure they learned—without severe injury or worse—from their mistakes on campus. It was a constant challenge.

I've learned through the years that we can never be sure that what our children do—good or bad—was *because* of what we did as parents or *in spite* of it. We do the best we can, we keep learning, we admit our mistakes, and we try again. We don't take all the credit for their success or all the blame for their failure.

I take promises seriously. In fact, it's one of the few things that will get me to the gym early in the morning! If I tell someone I'll be there—they can count on that. So please trust me when I offer these promises.

I promise you'll know more about how college really works than you did before (unless you work in higher education). I promise you'll know where to get more information and what help is available as you move through this. I promise you'll have tools to make better decisions about supporting your college-age students. You'll also get tools to keep yourself from becoming the dreaded "helicopter parent." I promise you'll have new ways to look at choices available to your student. I promise to offer a new perspective on being a successful parent of a college-age student.

Maybe you think you don't need this book yet because your child is only 13. Maybe you think it's too late because your child already flunked a semester of college and lost scholarships. I dispute both ideas in this book.

If you wait too long, you'll get caught up in the confusion of planning for college. Too much information will be thrown at you and your student to even keep track of. The saying "trying to get just a sip of water from a fire hose" comes to mind.

It's much better to prevent and prepare than it is to fight, freeze, or flee! (I just love a good chance to use alliteration.)

Start reading now and talk with your student—if **and only if** they're open to it. If not, pushing the issue will only make things worse. If they're not ready and willing to talk about it, talk with other parents in the same situation. They're everywhere.

Start a "book club" and find a way to have a positive support group (and wine, if that's your thing). It could take you through many challenges! This book can be a good guide and release a river of ideas.

Get out a pen and write in this book. Underline, circle, or put an arrow next to passages that really speak to you. Some people work better writing in a journal or typing their thoughts, especially if they're reading an electronic version.

This is a book I'd like you to not just read, but also interact with. Some things might not ring true to you, and that's valid. Just know I'm not making any of this up (reality is stranger than fiction), and I'm here to help.

There are almost always counselors in high schools who are paid to help your student prepare for college. They go by different names, and some schools have more and better resources than others. Some schools do a fantastic job with this. Others are overwhelmed by a huge number of students, or by student attitude or tough economic circumstances. However, there just aren't as many resources out there for parents!

If you hear about "helicopter parents" or—the new version—lawn mower parents, and don't want to be one of those, this book is for you.

What's the difference?

Helicopter parents are said to be overparenting, hindering their sons' and daughters' social development. They seem overprotective or overly invested in a child's life and feelings. They hover, monitoring and attempting to control a child's every move.

On the other hand, a *lawnmower parent* is one who clears a path for a child, a parent who intervenes in a situation before his or her child can experience any inconvenience or discomfort. They often continue the behavior once the child starts college, and often beyond.

There's plenty of good reading out there on this topic, if you want to see whether your own behavior might earn you this label. And while I'm not a huge fan of labels, our society is quick to use them.

Even if you feel you've made mistakes up to this point, it's not too late to learn and change. After all, that's what we're all hoping our children will do. Let's show them how.

I look forward to hearing what you get out of this book, and what you still need to know or understand better. There are answers out there, and people—including me—who want you to find them! Read on and connect when you're ready.

Becky Adair
Becky@Not13thGrade.com

How to use this book

There's no way for me to write this book and offer useful advice without using stories. Not all of these are my own stories, and where a real name is used with a story, I have permission.

There are so many people who've been part of this journey with me and have taught me ways to look at situations and people. Many of them had dramatically different experiences and a variety of strategies for handling them.

I wasn't the typical age for a Hall Director and didn't have the usual background. If you're wondering what the typical age and background would be, I'd say that most of the ones I worked with were in their mid- to late-20s (or maybe early 30s) with a master's degree in something related to students in higher education. I also worked with many who were working on a master's degree, and they would usually supervise a smaller dorm and have fewer official "office hours."

What is the job description of a Hall Director? Here's what I have on my work summary that I prepared for job applications. This describes the position I started in the summer of 2000.

As full-time, live-in professional staff, responsible for managing the day-to-day operations of the various programs and services in a 470-student, mostly freshman Residence Hall community with the goal of developing a positive community environment that supports the academic goals of the students and the mission of the University. The position requires seasoned judgment to provide direction and support in the form of advisement of the Resident Assistant (RA) staff and their programs, execution of crisis management and policy enforcement, and building maintenance. Use student development theory and strategies to provide an environment in the residence halls that enhances academic, personal, and social development in the residents. Teach classes to train and select RA staff.

In fact, I think one reason I got that first position was because they let my parenting and overall life experience substitute for what some of the younger Hall Directors learned in grad school.

Eventually, I would need that master's, but I was able to step in thanks to their generosity and desperation. To this day, I'm thankful that the University of Wyoming also didn't require a master's degree and helped pay for the one I got while working there.

In the following stories, sometimes characters are combinations of several people, the way movies often do. I hope they serve the purpose of providing a real-life example you can use.

A friend and former boss of mine, Sue Foster, sent me a copy of a speech she once gave. It was at the beginning of training for the live-in staff at her university, and it was full of amazing stories. She told them so the students would get a glimpse of what was ahead, and know it was something they could learn from and even enjoy. A couple of the stories I was there to experience with her, and I still shake my head in disbelief.

One of her wisest comments (and there were many) was this: "Never underestimate the power you hold to educate and influence others." It's a tough, intimidating call to action for a group of undergraduate students! And it's dead-on accurate. For the students **and** for the professionals.

Not all of it's serious, though. For example, Sue told of a time one of her Hall Directors received an urgent call from a mother at 7:30 on a Saturday morning. Mom was upset because her son's roommate didn't fold his clothes before placing them in his dresser drawers. That's one we just have to laugh about.

Quite a bit of what I've learned has happened since leaving the live-in role.

After 11 years of living on campus as part of my job, my husband and I returned to Texas to be with family and get a house off campus again. Our timing was perfect, as Texas A&M was starting up a new major project—the Academic Success Center. I was one of the first two Academic Coaches hired for this adventure and spent some time filling in the gaps I had around study skills and academic requirements.

One of the first things I learned was that even at a competitive-admission school such as Texas A&M, many students showed up without enough study skills. They needed immediate help with time management. Many weren't sure of their major, and some didn't even really know why they were in college, except that it was expected of them.

Because most of those who had appointments with us were there because of grade problems, most of them also needed to learn how (and when and where) to study. Most of all, they needed to learn that college isn't 13th grade.

This book also mentions further reading I recommend. Even though there are some wonderful books with helpful information, I remind you to make sure the right person is reading the right book!

For example, a book on study skills isn't going to do a parent much good—unless that parent is also a student. Your son does not want to learn about studying from you, unless he **specifically asks for your help**.

Handing your 17-year-old son the book, *That Crumpled Paper Was Due Last Week*, and hoping he'll get organized is a huge mistake. Read the book for what it can teach **you** as a parent.

Remember, it's hard enough to change ourselves, even when we want to. It's so much harder—and almost always impossible—to change others. Even when they *want* to change.

If your son comes to you and says, "I really need help with school—I'm already falling behind," then you can step in. But only a little at a time.

It's way too easy to jump in and try to become an academic coach. You may want to save him from himself and feel like a heroic parent at the same time, but that's a slippery slope. I know, because I slid down it like Clark Griswold on a snowy hill. (If you don't know that reference, I recommend that you watch *Christmas Vacation* before you finish this book.)

Keep in mind that I was an Academic Coach—a paid professional at a top four-year university—when my son left home for his first semester of college. I had so much to offer him! Study tips. Test strategies. Note-taking tricks. I even custom-made a planner for him (and his girlfriend) and had them printed. Complete with important dates for each semester already on the calendar for his college.

Those are hours and dollars I'll never get back and that he never used. Just know that you must be clear about *your* role, and *his or her* role. This must be about the student—**not** about you.

Even if you're paying for it, it's still about them.

I hope you finish this book and keep it on hand to look at again. I hope you loan it to a struggling relative or friend, or one who's looking at an 11th-grade daughter and wondering what's next. I hope you consider reading it with a group of friends who are in the same spot. I also hope you let me know what worked for you, and where you need more help. I hope you send me points and tips I didn't include. Any way we can find to help college-age students and everyone around them is a great idea in my book.

How this book can help different groups

Let's talk about what this book is **not**. It's not an academic thesis. As much time as I spent working in higher education and taking graduate courses in adult learning and counseling, I'm not a researcher or certified expert on any topic.

In fact, as much as I respect high-quality research in child development, parenting, and higher education, I loathe doing it. I know part of that stems from my deep-seated hatred of proper citations, and the way we're required to plop them into perfectly good sentences.

I do not for a minute claim that this book is well-researched in the standard sense. It isn't produced to academic standards by any means, other than correct spelling and punctuation and good (yet conversational) grammar. (That's not negotiable.)

I can't claim that science will back up what I'm recommending. Nor are my observations done in a lab, or in any kind of approved study. It's simply what I saw and experienced. As I said, I find **real** research difficult to read, even though I somehow got an "A" in a graduate-level research and statistics course. I also know statistics can be misused, and you can almost always find something to reinforce what you want to believe is true.

My experience is limited to two different public four-year universities and one non-residential community college (in three different states) and many different students, but still isn't a "representative sample" of the thousands of higher education institutions.

However, I've lived, cooked, and traveled with students. I've hired them, fired them, danced with them, cried with them, laughed with them, hugged them, applauded them, questioned them, sung (badly) with them, played board games with them, watched movies with them, taught them about Blue Bell ice cream, driven in the snow with them, high-fived them, shared awards with them, met their parents, welcomed their siblings, watched them get married, opened my home to them, colored with them, avoided tornadoes with them, shopped with them, referred them, coached them, advised them, done workshops for them, loaned them my car for a road trip, done presentations with them, dressed funny with them, planned with them, edited their résumés, exchanged gifts with them, been injured in front of them, worried about them, done stupid cheers with them, argued with them, done challenge courses with them, supported their coming out, bought matching shirts with them, named stuffed animals with them, cleaned mountain cabin bathrooms with them, learned from them, and listened to their struggles and excitement at all times of day and night. I've had them come to me eagerly for advice, and I've had them come to me only because they had to, or they'd be kicked out of school.

Critics can point out that my experiences are becoming more out-of-date each year. My first full-time position in a residence hall started in 2000. So much has changed in higher education, as well as in high school and before. So much has been impacted by social media and society in general. But some basic things don't change that much.

People in higher ed must react swiftly to new laws, new expectations from students, new levels of involvement from parents, new graduation requirements, and new mandated training. That includes such things as active shooter training, which I first did the year after the Virginia Tech shootings in 2007.

Please keep the timeframe of my experiences in mind as you read and choose what fits for your current situation. While I hope to update this book as things continue to change, I can't control which version you're reading.

Here's where I'll give you some background on myself as a parent. I think it's relevant, so bear with me.

I started my first full-time job on a university campus in 1987. Someone born that year is over 30 now and could be dealing with elementary-aged children. Their experience as parents is probably vastly different from my own. Which leads me to another disclaimer about my "credentials" to write this book.

I had only two kids with my first husband Mike, and they were eight and four when we split up. We chose to coparent them, and there was constant and free-flowing access. But he lived with them day-to-day. I picked them up from school a lot because my schedule was more flexible. He had always been the one to take them to pediatrician appointments, though, because he always had more sick leave. He was, without a doubt, much more of a "natural" at parenting babies and small children.

As my kids got older, I got a little better at it, and that probably had to do with fewer bodily fluids needing to be handled. I get my squeamish nature from my mother, and it hasn't changed over the years.

When Mike and I divorced, we decided the kids would stay in their house with him and keep going to their neighborhood school. I received plenty of criticism for this decision. The same kind I got when I'd travel for business during our marriage. People would say to me, "Who's with your kids while you're out of town?" I was floored when they didn't understand my response of "Their father." How is it that I'm such a horrible mom just because he's such a terrific dad?

All these years later, I see more and more stay-at-home dads, and that makes me happy! Mike and I would have gone that route if I'd made enough money to cover both our salaries.

Oddly for women my age, I loved going back to work after my kids were born. At the office, I usually knew what I was doing. Our kids loved their high-quality day care, always eager to be there yet just as eager to see us at the end of the day. I was excited, not crying, on the first day of kindergarten. They went to a wonderful school with education professionals who loved teaching and were good at it. Staying home with me would have been a disaster for all of us!

I'm not here to argue the point about who should stay home or for how long. That must be decided by parents, based on the choices and resources available to them. They must design a parenting scenario that works best in their world, based (I hope) on who has the best temperament for being with small children all day.

Some people don't have a choice, and I'm not well-informed enough to argue effectively about why that is. It would invariably get into economics and politics—two classes in which I got a "D" at college.

I share this so you'll know that I'm not the typical stay-at-home mom, or a typical work-outside-the-home mom either.

My kids grew up having a room with bunk beds in a residence hall on an enormous college campus, in addition to their own rooms at their dad's house. They went trick-or-treating with my staff and helped update bulletin boards for the Resident Advisors (RAs). They spent a great deal of time around college students, and probably heard some things I'd rather they didn't. But they also met some amazing young people and saw what college was about from the inside. When I moved 1,000 miles away to Wyoming when they were 11 and 15 (for a promotion into another kind of live-in job) it added a whole new dimension to their experiences.

In this book, I share my observations, express my concerns, and offer some solutions I think could make a difference. There's certainly not one right answer to any of this.

Many people are writing about this topic. Most of the books focus on showing parents how to guide their students through college, how to learn to enjoy the (temporarily) empty nest, or how to make sure their kids get into the "right" schools. I touch on the first two and completely avoid the third, except I refer you to financial guru Dave Ramsey and his opinion about elite colleges and going into debt for them.

Several good books are out there that will tell you what to expect when your "child" goes off to college, and I offer a list of the ones I think are best at the end of this book. Again, read them with the intention of being informed as a **parent.** Not with the intention of telling your student how to do everything. **They will not hear you!** You might as well throw seeds onto concrete and hope flowers grow.

Even when your children **ask** for your advice, they often ignore it. When they're not asking, they will *definitely* ignore it. They'll listen more to their peers, which isn't a new phenomenon.

The challenge of parents and orientation

One of the biggest challenges at most schools is putting together a new student orientation that students will absorb and use. They seem to need so much information, and it's offered to them at full blast.

Meanwhile, in *their* separate sessions, first-time college parents are soaking up all that's said, hoping their student is doing the same in their sessions. I promise you—most aren't.

The experienced parents are either not there or are more than happy to provide you with the **real** story. Listen to them, but make sure you have that grain of salt ready (and a margarita, if that's your thing).

Don't get me wrong. Orientation can be done well. And the students who are eager to be there and who have decided they aren't "too cool for school" will learn a lot! They'll make some valuable connections, they'll know where to go for help, and they'll hit the ground running.

They're the exception, though.

As much effort, time, and money as colleges put into orientation, they get even more frustration out of it. It can feel as if nobody is listening, and students are just in the room because it's required. It's incredibly disheartening to be that presenter when you **know** what you're offering will make a difference.

You also know that the students—or really the parents—will be asking questions you've already answered. That continues all semester.

Here's where my first pet peeve comes from.

The parents are asking the questions.

Not the students.

The students are usually rolling their eyes, texting their friends, and wondering how much longer it's going to take.

The ones with overbearing or controlling parents are either embarrassed or so used to it that the student just goes along with it.

These parents (at least one of them) have been doing this for **years**.

The students don't bother to speak, even when they're asked a direct question. They know mom will answer anyway. I remember feeling sorry for those students, and hoping they'd find their own voice in college. It was doubtful, but there's always hope.

One source of that hope, at least in the eyes of a college employee, is FERPA (Family Educational Rights and Privacy Act). If you've had a college student already, you've heard of FERPA. Here's a link to the official definition and what you most need to know: https://tinyurl.com/y4uws3pv

It all boils down to this: once your student turns 18, you no longer have easy and constant access to their grades (or much else) without their written permission.

It's federal law.

FERPA isn't something colleges invented so they don't have to talk to you. Faculty can't even confirm that your student is registered for a class, much less tell you whether they've been attending. So, if your student is having a problem, your **student** needs to get help!

Countless full-time professionals are available on campuses of all sizes to help students. New positions have been invented in recent years to provide even more assistance.

When I gave the parent presentation at a Tennessee community college during orientation each summer, I listed at least four people that each student could contact directly on campus who are getting paid to help.

That's their **whole job**—to make sure students succeed.

But the students will not succeed if mom and dad are trying to solve everything **for** them.

We used to jokingly say, "What are the parents gonna do next—go with them to job interviews after graduation?" Turns out, that's no joke. These are the helicopters and lawnmowers.

Parents are going to interviews, helping negotiate for a raise, and protesting the loss of a job. I haven't personally witnessed that, so it's anecdotal evidence. But I've heard it and read about it in some reputable places. (It's worth a Google!)

However, I *have* had conversations with parents who wanted to handle roommate conflicts for the student. These students, by the way, never reported any kind of conflict to me or to their RA who lived a few doors down from them.

I've had parents insist that an attorney be present for a discussion about roommate problems. I told one parent that any student with a roommate problem was more than welcome to come talk with me in my office or my apartment (both in the dorm). She told me her student didn't handle things like that—*she* did. Therein lies a big part of the problem!

Back before "smart" phones, roommates usually had to talk to each other…eventually. These days, they'll text or post on Snapchat what their gripe is, and they might even be sitting in the same room when they do it. They'll call mom to complain about something they've never *mentioned* to the roommate. Mom will then call the Vice President—especially if mom is a donating alum.

I've had parents demand the vice president's phone number when I told them I couldn't discuss a student issue with them. Our Vice President at A&M was more than happy to have us give out his direct line. He would repeat what I told the parent, and carefully explain the process just as I had. It's nice when the powers-that-be have your back!

One of my favorite stories about someone "up high" having my back happened in Wyoming.

My dorm housed all the freshmen football players (this was a smaller Division 1 school), and I was new to the school. One of them had been caught smoking marijuana in his room (trust me, we can smell it over the Febreze™).

My RA wrote up an incident report, which then automatically came to me. As I'd been trained to do, I forwarded it to the coach. Coach called me at my hall office and said, "Let me give you my cell number. If any one of my guys steps out of line in your dorm in the future, I want to know about it right away. He'll work a whole lot harder for me that week, I promise you!"

The freshman linebacker ducked his head to get into my office, then squeezed himself into one of my chairs so we could discuss the incident.

His first words were, "I'll do whatever you tell me to do—*just don't tell Coach!*"

It's amazing how quickly word spread of the consequences of breaking rules (and laws) in the dorm. I know it's not like that at most Division 1 schools—especially with football. In fact, at many schools, the athletes aren't required to live in a dorm as freshmen. Some because there isn't enough room, and some for reasons I'm sure I don't understand. That's a whole 'nother book!

But having the backing of a head coach gave me leverage that nothing else could.

Speaking of football players, here's another story. I got "voluntold" to do a presentation for the incoming freshmen one year. I was asked to tell them about living in the dorms and what all that meant.

In a room full of large young men, one slightly smaller one came up to me and shook my hand. This cocky future quarterback said, "My name's Austyn, and I'll try not to be too much of an asshole." He must have done some growing up because, not long ago, he was chosen to be the first-ever director of character and culture development as a coach at an SEC school.

Helping parents and other supporters

Parents are my main target audience for this book because I can relate best to them. Also, because they might be the only group willing to listen! But it's not really a good idea to lump all parents into one category—a lesson I've had reinforced recently.

While working at a typical four-year public institution, I usually saw stereotypical parents. They were often:
- in their early 40s
- had attended college (some had graduated)
- had full-time jobs (at least one of them)
- had more than one child
- were affluent (at least not struggling financially)
- lived in some version of the suburbs
- wanted at least that much for their kids

This description was even more true at Texas A&M, where many of them were also Aggies (if not second-generation Aggies who married Aggies).

That's not to say we didn't also see parents who had not attended college, or single parents, or parents with only one child, or parents who lived in the country or the heart of the big city. I'm just describing the kind I saw *most* often.

At the University of Wyoming—the only four-year institution in that state—it was a little different. We saw a lot of parents who lived in Colorado and just flat out didn't want to (or couldn't) pay the tuition there. It was less expensive back in the early 2000s to pay out-of-state tuition in Wyoming than in-state tuition in Colorado.

We also saw more parents who ran a ranch or lived in a *very* small town. That's just the nature of Wyoming. We saw a lot of Mormon parents as well (or LDS, as they call that population up there).

Speaking of LDS, here's quick story about cultural differences that showed up when I moved from Texas to Wyoming.

On the drive from the Denver airport to Laramie for my interview, my host asked me if we had a lot of LDS in Texas.

I realized quickly how much Star Trek had influenced my world. All I thought of was Captain Kirk telling someone in 1980s San Francisco that Mr. Spock had "done a lot of LDS in the '60s."

Turns out, LDS in Wyoming means Latter Day Saints. Which, of course, we had fewer of in Texas because it wasn't as close to Utah as Wyoming is.

Over a decade later, once I arrived in the Middle Tennessee region, I learned that the three stars on the flag stand for the three regions (East, Middle, and West). I also met more parents who had not attended college.

Part of the reason for that difference is that I was working at a community college that didn't offer bachelor's degrees. They offered associate degrees and certificate programs.

Many of the parents at Volunteer State Community College were just hoping their students would get some sort of college and break out of the cycle of poverty they'd grown up with. I also met plenty of parents who were students themselves. It was wonderful to hear them say, "I raised my kids, and they got to go to college, so now it's ***my*** turn!"

For all these kinds of parents, and others I didn't list, I wrote this book so you might find some new ways of looking at your role. Maybe you'll get some new understanding of how to support your student without smothering them. It could be that you know more about coaching your student through this experience than you think, no matter how much formal education you have.

Many students today are facing this journey with supporters who aren't their biological—or adoptive—parents. They might have foster parents or lost their parents in some way. That could be death, imprisonment, or complete disconnection.

Luckily for them, a relative, friend, or mentor has stepped up in that support role, and that person wants to know more about being on their team. I've met uncles, aunts, grandparents, godparents, older siblings, and family friends who wanted to make sure that this young person they care about has the best and most support available. So, this book is for them as well.

I'll never be someone who tells another parent how to do that job. It's one of the hardest and most rewarding jobs many of us are offered the chance to do. And many people stumble into it!

Many more aren't prepared for it, or not well suited to it. But they do it anyway because that's what good parents should do. It must be done, and none of us have it all figured out.

With any luck, they aren't surrounded by people criticizing and judging their efforts. Sadly, today's society is full of critics—especially on social media. We are way too quick to judge a parent's choices, even when we don't know what their options were or what they faced when they decided. It would make so much difference if we could be supportive, understanding, and empathetic instead. I know there are books out there about that topic as well!

So, this book isn't as much a "how to" book as it is "hear my story then consider this" book. It's offered to parents from someone who has been on the inside of both parenting and college and has seen so many ways ***not*** to do it.

I hope my observations give you some additional insight, some new choices, and some excellent resources. At the very least, I'm offering you a lot of truth, a little humor, and some help.

Helping students

Students are the heart of this book, but probably the least likely to pick it up, much less read it and make changes based on it. But, as an optimist, I'll write to them as well.

What can students get out of this book? I've called on the best resources to help me write this book: other students. Some of these students did things right and did it from their first days on campus. Others did things well, but only after making mistakes. Sometimes, they asked for help to recover from those mistakes. Other times, that took a while!

Some still haven't learned enough to make them successful at college. But they haven't given up hope that someday it'll be the right time to get more education. Some of them figured out that they could do something useful, interesting, and legal that they enjoy—and make a good living—without finishing college.

One thing I learned from students is that they're most likely to listen to other students, not to people wearing a name tag who are older than dirt, like me. That's okay—if they verify the information and choose the best students to listen to.

That's often where things go wrong.

Too often, students listen to rumors and take them as fact. They also fail to ask whether the student who's telling them how to do things has been *successful* in that area.

If you want to make good grades in Engineering, for example, don't ask a student in the Fine Arts how to do that. Not that an art student can't make good grades in Engineering, but there are vastly different kinds of exams, projects, and expectations. Usually, art students excel in some areas that an Engineering student probably won't. That's not always the case, and it's just one example, but I've known very few successful Engineering students who hated math, and very few Music majors who weren't creative in that way. It's a matter of fit, strengths, and aptitude.

There **are** people out there who have natural ability in Engineering and do well in Business, have a heart for Counseling, and communicate in a way that would make a Journalism major proud. I know this because I'm married to one! Some of it came naturally to him. Other parts took a little more work and didn't happen as quickly.

I hope students will consider how much time I've spent with college students. My passion was coaching them to succeed at what they most want out of life.

One of my favorite stories is about a student at Texas A&M who was required to meet with an Academic Coach because of his grades. The minute he came into my office—late for the appointment—I could tell he really didn't want to be there. He was rude, disrespectful, and sarcastic. He clearly wasn't listening.

Very quickly, I knew we were wasting time. Because I knew my boss had my back, because nothing good was going to come from our time together, and because I had other things to do, I decided to level with him.

I said, "It's clear you don't want to be here right now, so why don't we just check the box that says you came to see me, and you can go do what you'd rather be doing. I can get something done for someone who *wants* to learn with a coach."

He was surprised, and just stared at me for a few seconds. I sat in the silence, as I'd been trained to do, and he finally got up and left. All he said as he left was "Whatever."

About a month later, I saw his name on my schedule of appointments. I didn't know what to expect, so when he showed up (on time), I said, "Howdy, come on in," and just waited.

His first words were, "I owe you an apology. I was a real asshole last time I was here, and you don't deserve that."

I responded with, "Well, I'm not sure I'd give you that label, but you sure didn't want to be here. So why are you here now?"

With an embarrassed smirk, he said, "Well, when I got a 20 out of 100 on my exam, I knew what I was doing had to change. I'm here to learn how to study, if you're still willing to show me."

It would have been easy to give that young man an "I told you so." But somehow, I kept that to myself (an ability that comes more often with age). Instead, I smiled and said, "Let's get started!"

Helping higher education employees

I use the word "employees" here because I've always hated it when people said "Faculty, Staff, and Administrators." Technically, we all worked for the college or university. Yes, there were different levels of privilege, pay, and expectations. But the paychecks all came from basically the same place.

In some way, all employees in higher education are there for the students. Even those who don't spend a lot of time face-to-face with students are doing work that *impacts* students. I've been in several of those jobs and offices, including:
- Public Relations (even though we couldn't call it that)
- Human Resources
- Admissions & Records
- Publications
- Residence Life & Dining
- Academic Success Center
- Advising Center

That reminds me of something that happened in a classroom.

I was a full-time employee taking classes toward my master's degree (that ended up taking 26 years from start to finish). I was in a graduate-level marketing class, focused on human resources. All the other students were in their 20s, having recently completed a bachelor's degree somewhere.

For some reason I can no longer remember, the discussion compelled me to ask this question of the class: "Other than professor or football coach, can you name any other jobs that people hold on this campus?"

They were only able to come up with custodial staff, food service, bus driver, and campus police. Even having spent at least four years on a college campus, they were unable to come up with any more from what's a **huge** list!

A college campus, as you may know, is a town in and of itself. A **small** town, in some cases, but it has almost all (if not all) of the roles to be filled that a small town would have. The students in the class just had never considered it and had never considered *working* on a college campus!

As higher ed professionals know, the list of jobs is almost endless, and the environment is different from working out in the "real world."

How is it different? You think in semesters. You might love working with students, but you look forward to winter break so you can go to a movie at a local theater without standing in line. You realize that you get older each year, but those new students are always about 18. You wish the students understood that 8 a.m. and 5 p.m. aren't the best times for them to try to enter or leave campus unless they must, because you are **required** to! You often find yourself thinking, *Wow—when I was in college, it was a lot different!* Even if it's the same college.

These things are heightened for those in Student Affairs (or Student Services, or whatever a school calls it). Especially for those who "live in" or "live on." I didn't know there was a difference, by the way, but there is. I lived **in** because I lived in a dorm with the students. The Vice President for Student Services lived in a house on campus with just his family when I was a student at Texas A&M. He lived **on**.

I must stop here because the man I just referred to recently passed away, at age 89. Dr. John J. Koldus was Vice President when I was a student at Texas A&M, and he was truly beloved.

He was famous for his student gatherings, and for telling you that if he met you a second time and didn't remember your name, he'd buy you lunch. He meant it, but rarely did he have to buy anyone's lunch. He had such an impact that they named an important building after him—while he was still alive—based on students insisting that it be done.

They gave him a reserved parking space in that building's parking garage, in the heart of campus, after he retired. This is a man whom many considered a mentor and guide. Aggies for decades knew, respected, and cherished him. He will be missed by many. As Aggies do, I (and thousands of others) will answer "Here" on his behalf when his name is called at Aggie Muster in April 2020. He was the definition of impact.

Back to why I hope this book helps you, the employees.

I hope it's something you're willing to share with parents you encounter. I'm hoping it gives you tips for navigating some of the tougher situations you might encounter in your day-to-day work on a college campus. I hope it reassures you that what you're seeing is really happening, it often makes no sense, and things really do need to change. I hope it ultimately gives you some tools that make you realize how special the profession you've chosen is to the future.

It's tough to explain what you do to relatives at Thanksgiving, but when you meet a fellow higher ed person—you know they get it. And you can joke with them about people thinking you get summers "off."

Regardless of your role on campus, I hope you see some of your reality in this book. I hope you find some new ideas and solutions to what you're (under)paid to deal with. The ideas aren't all mine, by any means. I'd love to hear your stories for updates to this book—if the main point of your stories is to **help**!

Helping high school counselors

There are some wonderful high school counselors out there and some who should probably consider doing something else. The good ones can truly help guide a student to some valuable choices of what's next after high school, and the others can completely derail the education that a student goes to next.

It's easy to blame someone at the high school. But they're having to do **much** more crisis counseling and mental health counseling than career counseling.

Meanwhile, I can say that many students here in Middle Tennessee are strongly encouraged to go to college because they can get two years for free. They need only apply, graduate from high school, do eight hours of community service per semester, maintain a 2.0 (C) average, and go to a few meetings.

In theory, it's a great idea to offer students their first two years without having to pay tuition. Of course, they still must pay the outrageous prices for textbooks that get rewritten with a few new paragraphs every two years. So, counselors are urging them to make the most of this opportunity. I can't fault them for that.

I've often wondered what "directives" were given to high school counselors when it came to how many of their students went to college. Because it's become somewhat of a numbers game in many places. They, too, may be facing those expectations.

What do I mean by that? At my final job in higher ed, we received much of our funding based on **completion**. That word was even in my title (Completion Advisor).

Students had to enroll to be counted. Then they had to attend a certain amount to get financial aid (and for the school to be able to count them on census day—the magic day for funding). Then they had to make the grades to pass the classes. Finally, they had to graduate. That's considered **completion**.

There's no funding awarded for the students I could convince that college was a bad fit—even if it would make them happy and it was true. That didn't mean they weren't intelligent or hard-working. It might have just meant the timing was wrong, or they were only going to college to please someone else. How I wish I had a dollar for every time I heard that and knew it was real.

Just know that I strongly believe that many people shouldn't go to college.

For some, it's a matter of timing or attitude. For others, it's a matter of aptitude. For most, though, it's an issue of fit, and of society undervaluing professions that don't require a college degree. Could high school counselors have this kind of discussion with students? I'm not sure what they're "allowed" to say at this point, but it seems helpful to me.

Many people are best suited to jobs that don't require a *minute* in a college classroom and prefer them. And they're honorable professions that people like me (with a master's degree) will gladly pay someone else handsomely to do. Because it's something I **can't** do!

Of course, there are plenty of jobs that require a great deal of education and training. An obvious one is physician (or "medical doctor," as my father used to say, because he had a Doctor of Jurisprudence degree. In other words, he was an attorney). I'm sure we could all name several more that clearly require certifications, degrees, and continuing education.

However, our world would be a scary place if we had to rely on people who **only** have a degree but have very little common sense or practical training. And I've met many. Their credentials are impressive, but their skills are limited. Their egos often get in the way of connecting with students.

At a community college, I didn't see that issue. However, I did see underpaid instructors (some with master's degrees, some with doctorates) who truly did care about learning and the people in the classroom.

However, one of their struggles was trying to teach a class where half of the students couldn't read at college level—much less write. It's even worse in the math classes. And when so many of the students are only sitting there because they're forced to (at least for some of the semester), it's a tough audience. When you're a subject expert who feels passionately about your topic, it can be incredibly discouraging.

I feel like a quick personal side story would help here.

My only direct experience as a classroom instructor was in teaching College Success to students whose ACT/SAT scores weren't high enough. They had to take a combo of college reading and college success. They **had** to take it before they could get into most of the courses they needed to get a degree.

I requested an in-person class (as opposed to online only) because I wanted a chance to meet them face-to-face, listen to them, share my enthusiasm for the topic, and help them do much better than the standardized tests said they could.

What I should have realized was that the curriculum was pretty much set in stone for consistency, and all their graded work was to be done on the computer. The classroom was mostly chairs in front of tables with computers on them. I bet you can guess what got most of their attention.

If they showed up at all, they clearly wanted to be *anywhere* else.

Rarely had they done any reading before class, much less the actual assignments clearly explained in the syllabus I went over with them on day one. They didn't take notes on anything I said in class. They didn't put any dates on calendars, because they didn't use them. At most, they'd put a reminder in their phone about a test. It was so frustrating for me every Tuesday and Wednesday night that semester—especially after working as a Completion Coach all day. I *so* wanted to help them.

The curriculum, the textbook, the materials online, and, especially, I wanted to give them the tools to be successful in college. Some of the tools would apply even if they didn't plan to attend beyond an associate degree. In fact, some of it would be helpful no matter **what** they chose to do with their adult life. But they just wanted to get through it, get credit just for showing up, get the grade they needed, and get done.

Of course, every class of 24 had a couple of students who really wanted to learn. They were there because it mattered to them, and they knew they would need help. I wish I had been strong enough to let their attitude make up for the others. I wasn't. It was just too discouraging.

I knew what most of them faced if they wanted to continue toward a degree, and it was obvious they weren't ready. It was also obvious they had never been allowed to fail and learn from it. I even told them that failure was fine with me. If I saw effort on the front end and learning on the back end, I gave them the chance to try again. I once asked them what they'd do differently given another chance after failing. The answer that broke my heart was, "Just choose a different answer."

I had already explained that when you fail a test or assignment, you must go back and see what went wrong. Could you have prepared differently? Did you read the wrong part of the book? Did the question confuse you? Did you second-guess your answer? There are so many things that could be corrected for the second try. They just weren't interested in that kind of learning.

I told them that unless they received a zero grade, they had done something right—and we could look at what **did** go well for them. Maybe that right answer was the topic they asked a question about in class. In that case, maybe they should ask more questions. Or perhaps it was the material they discussed with another student in a study group, or it was a problem they worked on at a desk instead of in bed.

There were so many ways to **learn how to learn**, and I was there to walk them through it. Most didn't want to take that walk. They wanted the degree without the work, and the high-paying job without the education to deserve it.

Many have grown up in a world where food can be microwaved, answers are on their phones, and trophies were given to everyone who showed up. This isn't a rant against the millennial students, though. They weren't the ones handing out the trophies.

We, as their parents, wanted them to be spared any pain, disappointment, or tears. We were told they needed to feel good about themselves, and if only the best got rewarded, that wouldn't happen.

I'm a big fan of self-esteem and not a believer in humiliation. I'm also aware that the word "discipline" means to *teach*—not to *punish*.

However, as many much smarter (and more research-based) authors will tell you, that effort went overboard. Not every child is an athlete or an artist. And that's **more than** okay. Not every adult is a surgeon, either. And I hope the surgeons are grateful for the mechanics, the plumbers, and the custodial staff who make their lives work.

By the way—some of those so-called "blue collar" workers are smart and well-educated individuals. Some just don't want to deal with the nonsense required to play the corporate game.

I once had the privilege of working with a custodian in a dorm who had a degree in Engineering. The students assumed he wasn't smart or educated, and many treated him as if he were beneath them.

Turns out, he had been an Engineer and got fed up with the "rat race," the hours, and the competition. He wanted a job he could do well, be proud of, and see definite results right away. He wanted to go home at night after a good day's work and not worry about the office.

How I wish those students had known that about him and given him the respect he deserved *regardless* of his degree. Even if he had only finished 5th grade, he deserved to be treated as an individual doing an honest job and doing it well.

Why have so many people forgotten the value of that?

There are countless people in the world who do jobs I know I can't do or don't want to do. I'm deeply grateful that they do them! It's even better when I can see that they enjoy their work and realize the value of what they offer.

So many wise and wonderful people have never stepped foot in a college classroom. My credit hours don't make me any better than them. In some cases, I've been embarrassed about what I can't do or don't know, and how much I need them. They sure don't need *me*, regardless of a framed diploma on my wall.

Sometimes, I feel like I'm "just another woman" who doesn't understand cars, or how to build something, or how to make my yard look amazing. I'm not ditzy or anti-feminist, but I know what I'm not good at. And it doesn't matter for a minute to me whether people whose help I need went to college. It matters whether they can do a job well that I'm ready to pay for. And I truly hope they enjoy what they do because when I try to do their job, I feel like an idiot.

Then again, there are many people in task-oriented jobs who would prefer to be in an office—but don't yet have the credentials. There are plenty of hard-working and smart people who can't or don't get to go to college right after high school. Sometimes it's not for *decades*. They should absolutely have access to a good education at affordable rates, and support throughout the process.

Tennessee recently introduced the "Tennessee Reconnect" program for adult students who don't have some sort of degree. They get the same tuition-free access offered to the high-school students, but they don't have to go full time. Mostly because the majority are working and/or raising a family.

Whenever I had a chance to help one of those students adjust to college—again or for the first time—it was incredibly rewarding. These students wanted to know anything I could tell them that would make their college experience go more smoothly.

They're willing to be in class every session, sit in the front, ask good questions, take effective notes, study far in advance, and continue to improve the way they do things. They recognize what they can get out of school and know what they need to put into it. And boy are they appreciative!

Not that any of us do the academic coaching job for the appreciation, but it's nice to get it every now and then. It's nice to know you've given someone a tool they need, and they actually use it. When they take the time to say thank you, or recommend you to another struggling student, it's a huge reminder about why you chose to do the job. For a few minutes, you feel like you matter. Like you've made a difference.

However, I've seen firsthand how being offered a "free two-year degree" can go wrong. Again, I haven't researched this, but I can tell you anecdotally that, many times, people don't value what they don't have to pay for. You can even see that in students whose parents pay for their whole education.

I've known many students who had to work their way through school and valued that education so much more. Of course, there's a balance there as well. Working too many hours leads to different problems.

Many experts say a student shouldn't work more than 20 hours per week if they're planning to be full-time which is usually defined as 12 credit hours. Students getting the tuition-free college in Tennessee must be enrolled for at least 12 credits per semester.

Academic advisors, however, recommend that students take 15 credit hours so they can finish an associate degree (or get half-way to a bachelor's degree) in two years.

Some students believe that they get the degree if they just keep enrolling for two years, regardless of the classes they take or the grades they get. Some think that if they're enrolled in Tuesday/Thursday classes, they get to choose which day to attend. They're also appalled to think that they have reading or class work to do outside of in-class time.

Those of us who went to "traditional" college in a "traditional" way often wonder how they could think those things! But there are many reasons why what we "just know" isn't something that would even occur to them. Here are a couple of examples of that.

There are many students whose parents didn't attend college (for a variety of reasons). College is never really a topic of conversation at their home because some parents don't want to talk about things that they're not familiar with. In homes where at least one parent attended college, those parents often just assume their children know these things. It's been so long since a parent didn't know that, they don't even remember a time they didn't. (There's even a name for that phenomenon, and it often applies to professors. It's called the "curse of knowledge.")

Even a good counselor in high school might not think to mention such details. She had to get a least a master's degree and it's now just an ingrained part of what she knows. To top it off, so many high school students just don't want to listen to adults lecture them about one more thing.

The exceptions, as I've seen, are the home-schooled and the competitive private school students. Much more is expected of these students, and different conversations take place at home and at school.

I've been in small-group meetings with high school students who plan to attend college simply because it's "free." I've also been in those meetings with students who are using community college to boost their GPA in basic classes, so they can transfer to a four-year school, ready to tackle the classes for their major.

Very different discussions take place in those meetings.

This second group is willing to give up the "freshman fun" and concentrate on getting an education. They want to learn how to be an effective student and avoid the party scene that sends so many students home sooner than expected.

It shouldn't have surprised me that students who realized the value of the "free" education and the academic coaching were the ones who didn't need as much help.

They had already learned how to use a planner. They knew it would take more than a few hours "going over their notes" the night before a chemistry test to do well in it. They were aware of the advantages of:
- sitting in the front row
- introducing themselves to professors before there's a problem
- taking good notes
- having read the assigned text before class

These students didn't really need our help but valued it and asked for even more suggestions. The ones who truly appreciated my role and my desire to help were the non-traditional students (known to us as "non-trads").

Too many non-trads started college right out of high school and bombed quickly. Or they never got a chance to attend because of financial challenges. Or they became parents much sooner than they had planned. So, when they got a chance later to get some sort of degree, they were more aware of how it could change their lives.

They had often been passed over for a promotion for someone with less experience. But that person could check the box that said, "has a college degree." They were able to look back at their behavior and performance as a freshman in college and realize they had been clueless. Many just went to college because it's what you do after high school. All their friends were doing it! And, more importantly, it gave them freedom from parental control.

These aren't good reasons to go to college, but they're quite common. It certainly applied to me when I was in college! Maybe some of this is helpful to high school counselors when they do get a chance to have this kind of conversation.

Helping society, especially future employers

How can one book help society at large? Sounds ambitious, I know. But I'm hoping we can find a way to have a positive ripple effect. In the same way students follow peers they admire, especially if they see those peers getting what they'd like to have for themselves, I believe parents can spread the word on what works.

Let me expand a bit on previous sections here, because it all overlaps a bit.

When I first thought of this category, I was really thinking of employers. But the more I thought about it, the more it grew in my mind to include the whole of American society. After all, our kids will be working in many different industries, surrounding us wherever we go. If we're influencing these "kids" to make better choices sooner, perhaps they'll make an even more positive impact in their workplaces and on all of us.

The point is the "helicopter" level of involvement—dare I call it interference—clearly didn't start when the "child" was 21. It's most likely been happening since elementary school if not sooner. I know it happens in high school, because that's something I witnessed. Here's an example.

There's a mandatory meeting for all graduating seniors who are planning to attend college if they plan to use the tuition-free program in Tennessee. More than once, I got to attend as a guest speaker on behalf of the college I worked at, and twice I attended as a volunteer Mentor.

Mentors could be any adult who wanted to act as a Mentor for these students, and we would typically get four to six students on our list. Even at the first meeting, some wouldn't show up (it was held at their school, right after school). Those who *did* show up were usually joined by at least one parent. The student would usually say nothing, ask no questions, and reluctantly participate in a planning activity when forced to. The parents were often taking notes, and frequently wanted me to stay after and answer questions.

At this stage FERPA isn't an issue yet, but I still can't really answer specific questions about their student (I don't have their information in front of me). So, there we stand, them asking while I try to answer to the best of my ability. Where is the student?

If they're anywhere nearby, they're glued to a cell phone. They appear to not have any interest at all in questions whose answers could make the path a **lot** easier.

The last time I attended, when we broke into our small groups, I made it clear to my Mentees what I'd be more than eager to do to help, and what I *refused* to do. Some of what I refused to do was in direct contradiction to what the main speaker had just said a Mentor *should* do.

What was that? It was providing reminders to the students about deadlines.

Why is that so bad? Well, it's not horrible. But they're already getting weekly emails (that many ignore) as well as a printed booklet with every possible Q&A, guideline, and requirement. There's a well-made and often-updated website for this. So, I don't see the value of an additional text from me just to remind them of deadlines.

Instead, I encouraged my mentees to start right away using a planner—not just their phone. They can remind *themselves* of deadlines and give *themselves* time to prepare.

In my second year as a Mentor I insisted on working only with home-schooled or private school students. It didn't surprise me that each of them said they were using a planner already. They even wanted to hear how to better use one in college. **Hallelujah**!

I thanked their parents for raising students who understood how to use such a tool, and for teaching them to ask their *own* questions.

Maybe I'm becoming too cynical, but I just don't think we should be doing so much for these students.

If they're old enough to do things they *want* to do, they're old enough to fix a lunch (and breakfast) for themselves, remember to take it to school, write down due dates, and follow the painfully detailed guidelines every teacher provides.

As I heard once when I had young kids, "No child ever died from missing just one meal."

In fact, they were more likely to remember it next time—because they were hungry! Discomfort is a true motivator!

Every time we drop everything, rush back home, and get a child's lunch that was left on the counter, we teach them that we're there to fix the slightest inconvenience in their world. We also usually end up late for work.

Same thing with telling them it's cold outside and a coat would be a good idea. Unless you live in states where it truly gets dangerously cold (which I've done), refusing to wear a coat will just make them uncomfortable for a while. Chances are, they'll choose to wear a coat next time, especially if we avoid the temptation for the "I told you so!"

I remember a wonderful parent educator, Mary, telling me and my then-husband about picking our battles in that area. We were talking about how our little girl wanted to dress, and how we didn't want to look like neglectful parents in public.

Mary said, "As long as the two adults are dressed reasonably, and Chelsea isn't in danger, people will know who is making the clothing decisions for the child. And they'll smile and realize you're probably picking your battles wisely."

That was one of many things Mary said that made a huge difference in our parenting, and I think it applies as they get older.

Some things just don't matter that much. It's appearance management. Let's stop and think about what could truly endanger our children and make those decisions our battlegrounds. Let's look at natural consequences, such as this example.

My son was told to put his bike in the garage at the end of the day so it wouldn't get stolen. He didn't listen. Guess what? It got stolen. Guess who no longer had a bike to ride?

Having that bike get taken off the driveway when he left it out was a good lesson. And he couldn't be mad at his dad or at me about it. That wasn't the last time he faced natural consequences that were painful for us to watch, because kids must keep learning.

The long-term decision-making part of your children's brains isn't even fully formed until their mid-20s. That's one reason auto insurance is so expensive for males under 25!

I keep making bad choices on occasion, and I've had **54 years** of natural consequences! Many of them hurt quite a bit. But, eventually, I learn from most of them. Which reminds me of one of my favorite sayings: "Take my advice—I'm obviously not using it!"

My point is, they'll keep learning long after we're there to teach in person. But if we're always there to rescue, what are they really learning? I believe they're learning that mom and/or dad will be there to take care of things, so why learn or change?

What I've seen that's even worse lately is going beyond rescue. It's what I'll call—for lack of a better term—*over-preventing*.

We see cartoons about kids surrounded by bubble wrap before they leave home, and we all laugh. But lately it seems to almost be normal.

As Completion Coaches at a community college, we were told that a big part of our job is to remove all barriers to student success. Reread that last sentence. **Remove** all barriers.

Let me know if you've found a world where all barriers have been removed for you as an adult. I have yet to find one.

By removing those barriers, are we just setting them up for huge disappointment later? Or are we going to keep hovering around them the rest of their lives, so we'll feel needed and they'll be protected? I just can't see that as being healthy.

If removing barriers is wrong in my view, what do I suggest instead?

Knowing that life will continue to give all of us barriers of different heights, widths, and depths, I suggest we teach children how to get over, around, or through them. I suggest we teach them how to look at the barrier, figure out what tools they have to deal with it, then take action to handle it.

Teach them to ask for help to deal with those barriers. In my world, help implies that they have a role as well! Help doesn't mean doing it **for** them. It might mean doing it *with* them. It might mean referring them to someone better suited to help. It might mean offering them additional tools they might not have even known to ask for.

We need to learn to say, "What have you already tried?"

When I had students come in for coaching—which often just meant they wanted to register for classes—I would ask them that. Way too often they'd say, "I haven't done anything. I thought you'd do it for me."

I would ask myself, "Wait—isn't this the generation that grew up with access to computers? Can't they at least look at our website, where almost every answer is written?"

Most of the time, I'd end up walking them through the process in my office and letting them know it would be more convenient for them to do it at home the next time. After that, I'd be happy to look it over to make sure they're on the right track.

Some of them liked that idea and were relieved to see it wasn't that difficult. Others just wanted me to do it. They didn't want to think about it, and they didn't want to make a mistake.

More than a few times, I had parents call to complain about the schedule their students chose. After trying to explain that FERPA prevented me from even acknowledging that their student met with me, I would try to talk them through what I'd tell a typical student in a similar situation (see—we **do** want to help).

The parents often didn't understand that it's the **student's** choice of what classes to take, whether to attend class, and how much to learn. The student **cannot** be the one who cares the least! They must care **at least** as much as the parent, but preferably more.

Consider a father and son, for example, at new student orientation, and it's time to choose the student's first semester schedule. The parents who impressed me the most were the ones who would say, "This is about you, Son. You go on into the coach's office and see what works best for you. I'm out in the hall if you need me."

I'd have no problem with that student wanting Dad to join us before the final "register" button was pushed. It's fine to want a parent's vote of confidence! But it's **not** the parent's decision! Students who struggle to do anything without calling Dad will continue that struggle if the parents keep stepping in to rescue.

When I talked with parents (without their students) as a group, I would ask them which phone call they'd rather get.

Do they want the phone call in which their daughter says, "Mom—help me—I'm so unhappy with my roommate! Can you call someone and get me moved?" or the one in which she says, "Mom—I'd like to rehearse what I'm planning to say to my roommate about what's bothering me, so I can see if we can work things out. If it doesn't work, I'm going to get the RA's help."

If you'd rather get that first call, you might want to look at *why* you want that call. Do you miss being needed? Do you not trust your daughter's ability to handle the situation? If not, why not? Do you need to be the supermom to the rescue?

Personally, I *loved* getting the second kind of call from my own daughter. I loved that she was capable, and I loved that she valued my opinion. I loved that she was willing to try and had the skills to do so. It didn't always work, of course, and our next conversation would be about what the RA suggested. It might even be her calling to say even *that* didn't work, and was it time to take things up the chain?

These are life skills that we all need.

I firmly believe that we should give our kids roots and wings, as well as tools. Yes, it's nice to be needed. But I assure you it's even more satisfying to watch them become capable adults and want to share that with you. It's fun to get a phone call from your college graduate daughter in her first full-time job just to thank you (and her dad) for teaching her how to speak for herself. She's making this call because she's so tired of seeing students who can't do that! It makes her job harder as a professional!

When did that kind of training start? If I recall, it started to take hold when we would be at a fast-food restaurant. She would want some ketchup for her fries and ask us for it. We would remind her that they have it at the counter, and she was welcome to walk up there and ask for it politely. She'd be in our line of vision the whole time, and we'd rehearse what to say. She'd handle it, just like she'd handled ordering her own food, and feel more capable. She reminded me recently that we also had them order their own "fancy Dr Peppers," ask for cherries, and call to ask for part-time jobs from our friends. She remembered these lessons and is grateful for them. She still tells other people these stories. It was a simple—but important—starting point.

Helping me

It feels more than a little selfish to say I'm writing this book for me, but I've gotta be real. For many years I've been told I should write a book—by a variety of people—and I'm finally doing it. One reason I'm doing it is tied to leaving higher education employment at the end of 2018.

After years on campus, I went from jobs that didn't interact with students to a job where I *lived* in the same building.

My first full-time job after college was in the Texas A&M University Office of Public Information (OPI). I'm pretty sure I got that job because the manager confused me with someone else. But it got me out of Baton Rouge, Louisiana and back to my beloved College Station, Texas.

I had missed so many things about Aggieland, and this job was going to pay me to live there and be part of publicizing what Texas A&M was doing. While we couldn't call it Public Relations back in 1987 (I'm not sure if that's still the law), that's essentially what we were doing. My first area of coverage (known as a "beat" in newspaper terms) was the College of Geosciences. All I knew about geosciences was helping my college boyfriend study for his rocks and minerals test.

I soon discovered it wasn't a bad thing that I didn't know about the sciences. My role at OPI was to find out what professors and students were doing on campus and write about it in a way that would be interesting to the general public. One of our targeted newspapers was the *Houston Chronicle*. It's my hometown newspaper, and the one my mother was reading every day. (My dad read *The Houston Post*.) We tried to get stories into magazines, too. One of my favorite achievements was getting a story about hotel fire systems into Southwest Airlines' *Spirit* magazine.

When my dear friend Kathie (and later Matron of Honor) left our office to give birth to my godchild Emily, I got to take over the beat she'd done so well. That included some of my favorite subjects, like psychology, sociology, and communication. That was so much more fun, and much more appealing to the general reader out there.

I learned so much about what went on behind the scenes at a large university, which I found fascinating, if not a little disturbing. Our office got the phone calls when a student died in an alleged hazing incident. We also took the calls when the athletic department faced scandal and quit answering their phones. This was the 1980s, and it was about to get ugly.

After about two and a half years in that office, I left to try working off campus. For a few months, I tried to love working in wedding catering for the nicest hotel in our town. That lasted until several of us quit when the General Manager came back from lunch to find all his stuff removed from his office.

I was hired away by a company run by a childhood friend's parents—Bride 'n' Formal. I managed the store until I couldn't take it anymore and I knew I belonged back in higher ed.

God was watching out for me because I soon found a position with the Texas Engineering Extension Service (TEEX) working as a publication editor. This was 1990, and computers were nothing like they are today!

We spent a lot of time taking aging printed materials used in training classes and bringing them up to the current decade. We did all the marketing materials for such groups as the Fire School, the construction training division, and much more. It was a different focus and a different audience, but I was back on my beloved Aggie campus. In fact, my office was in a building that had once been the football dorm. If those walls could talk! Later I ended up meeting and working with Hugh McElroy, Aggie class of '71. He lived in that dorm as the first African American to start on the Aggie football team. I did get to hear some stories!

That job was great for about a year, when an even better one came open working for the actual university again (instead of a System agency). The person who had left the advertised job had joined our office at TEEX and gave me all the inside scoop on how to get her old job. It wasn't a good fit for her, and it looked like something I'd love.

Soon, I was interviewing to be the communications professional for the university's HR office. I was offered the job during that interview. I watched the Director of HR panic and recover when I told him I was expecting my first child seven months later! If the employee newsletter went out to all 30,000 employees and retirees without missing a month, he had no problem with it.

This was 1991, so it was quite a challenge to get my computer and printer home (with all the diskettes it required). But it all worked out, and that Director retired soon after. Many changes happened when he left. Then we had an interim Director, then hired a new Director (whom I'm still in touch with). What an incredible learning experience for me! More than 25 years later, I'm still in touch with at least six of the people I worked with in that office. And not all just on Facebook!

By this point, I was discovering that I get bored easily in a job. The first year, I learn it; the second year, I improve on it; and the third, I'm ready for change. If that change can happen within an office I'm already in and enjoy, that's great! But in higher education, there's not all that much flexibility in changing or creating positions.

I also was ready to be part of a communications team, not be the entire team on my own. I applied for a job doing communications for the System level of Texas A&M (the umbrella over all the campuses and organizations in Texas that "belong" to A&M). It was a similar job at a higher level. Also, I was still learning how to manage things with a child at home (Mike and I were both working on campus).

I thought it would be a great change for me. I quickly learned that System Headquarters was a more formal atmosphere than what I wanted. There wasn't enough laughter in our day-to-day world. My dear friend (to this day) Debbie Nanz Bush was the bright spot in that office for me. We joked about snipers on the roof making sure our lunch hour was **exactly** an hour. To say things were uptight was an understatement. I was a little afraid of leaving that position after only a couple of months, but I knew in three weeks that it wasn't a fit for me.

Once again, I had a heavenly guide. I was led to a new position being created in an office that once employed another friend of mine. I had heard how wonderful the boss was, and I wanted to work for her. It was a position still in communications, but also requiring a lot of planning and organizing—two things I've always loved and been good at. I was hired to be Assistant to the Director in the communications office of Admissions & Records. In this job I would get to edit some famous (or infamous) publications. That included the inch-thick official undergraduate catalog and the commencement programs. The best thing? I would have much more contact with the world of undergraduate students.

In this role, in 1994, I met Linda. She became my son's godmother (he was born about a year after I started there). She and I also rescued my friend Debbie from the office I had just left.

I learned so much about admissions (but not as much about records)! I was responsible for providing the answers about A&M to those national publications that review all the colleges you can choose from. I got to robe dignitaries at graduation ceremonies. I got to watch courses being officially created. I got to make sure every single name and hometown was spelled right in the commencement program. I also got to do some fun publications, and my inner editor was delighted!

After a few years in that role, once again I was stymied by a lack of rapid change available to me and reached my level of "boredom" with a role. I moved to the Texas Transportation Institute Information & Technology Center (TTI-ITEC), where the real design work was done. I had the privilege of trying to lead and manage three very talented graphic designers and try to keep up with rapidly advancing technology. It was about this time we were just beginning to make DVDs to recruit students to Texas A&M, and the Internet was fairly new.

Unfortunately, my marriage was dissolving, and I wasn't very good at my job. I was too distracted and disappointed in where I'd ended up. I didn't devote myself to truly leading and taking care of the designers and their expensive projects. Even after I realized all that and apologized to everyone impacted, I still didn't feel like I could stay where I was.

About that time (1998), having spent more time around students, I was selected for an honor that would change my life and my career path for good.

Texas A&M does an amazing job of indoctrinating incoming students beyond the usual orientation. We have a much-copied program called "Fish Camp." It began in the late 1950s to teach new students what being an Aggie was all about—*outside* the classroom. It was optional for new students, and the "counselors" for Fish Camp also paid to be part of it.

It wasn't long before it was incredibly difficult to win a highly sought-after slot as a counselor, and they kept having to add more three-day sessions. I tried and didn't get chosen, but my roommate did.

Fish Camp was held a couple of hours away from campus, in a Methodist retreat center in Palestine, TX. By the time I was a student, each camp session was divided into several colors, and students were put into a color group. Those color groups were then named for an Aggie that had mattered in some way (past or present).

These namesakes have included Medal of Honor winners, successful scientists and industrialists, and professors.

As A&M kept growing, and more students were beginning college in the Spring semester instead of Fall, they added a similar camp for those students. It was called Howdy Camp, and they had a similar namesake structure.

By the time I was working at Admissions, they had started naming the camps for current faculty, staff, and administrators. They were nominated by students and selected by the overall camp directors (all student leaders).

Somehow, I got nominated by one of our student workers who also babysat for my two kids. I was suddenly surprised with the announcement that I was the namesake for Camp Downey (my married name), the yellow session of Howdy Camp. I was stunned, thrilled, and incredibly excited! I asked the two student directors for my camp how involved I could be, and they said, "As much as you want!"

They hoped I'd deliver a "campfire speech" to my camp's students. If I wanted to, I could attend meetings once counselors were selected and training began. I couldn't get enough of it all, and they loved how much I participated! They put so much into planning everything, starting with a theme for our camp. For a variety of reasons that I can no longer remember, we became "*Camp Downey—Charlie Brown Playground Under Construction.*" I started a huge collection of yellow items for the camp.

That time with the Camp Downey folks was my first taste of what it could mean to have a career that mentored, counseled, or advised a group of students. They actually *wanted* my guidance and my time and attention! It was heady stuff to be listened to, and to have my name on everything! It was my first real glimpse of Student Affairs and I was quickly hooked.

While things were exciting for me with the Camp Downey kids and what I was learning about myself, other parts of my life weren't so positive. I was facing the "perfect storm" of a dissolving marriage, career unhappiness, and discovery of my calling. I decided to quit my job, move into an apartment, and begin divorce proceedings.

No, the students didn't break up my marriage. They were just the catalyst for taking the leap my heart was craving.

My first husband Mike, 12 years older than I am, did an amazing job of finishing (and correcting) the parenting my own parents hadn't been able to do the way I needed. He taught me about unconditional love, and he showed me how to become who I wanted to be.

Other people also showed me possibilities I'd never considered. I had never really believed I'd be any good at such things as training others, making presentations, mentoring, or coaching. I seemed to be an introvert, but that was about to be revealed as just the safe place I'd been hiding. After all, I'd always been told I was the one who made the grades—my brother Eddie made the friends.

During the year I was attending Coach University, I met and married my current husband, Chuck. I continued to coparent with my ex-husband, as our marriage dissolved in a friendly fashion. I believe we hugged each other in the parking lot at the courthouse on the day it was all final. I still think so highly of him and will always hate the fact that my choices hurt him. I'll discuss the impact on the kids later. It's a big part of who I've become both personally and professionally, and a part of their college experiences.

Why should you listen to me?

There's probably as many opinions about college and parenting as there are parents and colleges. So why should my perspective be valuable to you?

As I mentioned in the introduction, I'm no expert—as far as credentials—on any topic. But if carefully observed and documented experience is important to you, I'm sure I can draw on that to be helpful.

Starting with the personal side, I'm a mother of two now-grown children, Chelsea (born in 1991) and Davis (born in 1995). These two didn't have a traditional childhood in many senses of the word. While plenty of young children are the product of a divorced household, few are also children of a mom who lives and works full-time in a dorm.

When they were in elementary school, I took my first live-in position in their hometown, at my alma mater. They grew up in a college town, but this was taking things to a new level!

The idea of college students and going to class wasn't unusual to my kids. Their dad and I had both worked for Texas A&M in some capacity since before we married. They spent time at various campus events, they came to our offices, and they often had babysitters who were student workers for us. They attended football and baseball games with the rowdy Aggie crowds and learned the Aggie War Hymn and all the Aggie yells at an early age.

In 1999 when the Bonfire tragedy occurred on campus, my daughter wanted to go out to the site. They were still doing search-and-rescue operations and she wanted to go see if maybe they'd found more students alive. She ended up talking with the media and learning some harsh realities of a huge and dangerous project. She had seen Bonfire burn successfully once before but had not realized that lives could be at stake. It was a tough time in Aggieland, and we were all impacted.

Chelsea's soon-to-be-stepbrother, who was in the Aggie Band as a freshman that year, was supposed to have been on that Bonfire stack when it fell. Adam called me around 6 a.m. to let me know he was okay and that he couldn't get hold of his dad to let him know. I had to ask why he *wouldn't* be okay. He said words I'll never forget. "Bonfire fell, and four Aggies are dead." By the time it was all over, 12 would be dead and 27 injured. By the grace of God, Adam's outfit in the Band had traded Bonfire work shifts with another group because they wanted more practice for the upcoming performance at the football game. That trade most likely saved his life.

I can't remember now whether my kids went with us to any of the memorial gatherings around the Bonfire collapse. But I know they weren't at the football game against the University of Texas a few days after it fell. Chuck and I had bought last-minute tickets to the game from a student who worked in the ticket office. That student had decided to go be with his family instead. Many people had that reaction to the tragic losses on campus.

We were on the 50-yard line, second deck—amazing seats. We saw a miraculous last-minute come-from-behind victory. We also saw a performance by our rival school's band that honored the Aggies in a way we couldn't have predicted. There wasn't a dry eye in the record crowd of 86,000+ that day.

So, it's safe to say that my kids had seen some of the realities of campus life long before they were supposed to start thinking about college. Growing up in a town that's defined by a major university is different in so many ways. In fact, many young people decide to go anywhere **but** that school, because they've had enough by age 17. Others can't think of anywhere else they'd even consider going, especially those who are children of Aggies!

How my upbringing was different

I didn't grow up in a college town. I grew up in Houston—about 100 miles from A&M. My father was an Aggie class of '48. My mom would have been an Aggie class of '50 but, back then, they didn't let women in.

Her two older brothers were in the Corps of Cadets at A&M, but she attended Texas State College for Women (TSCW) north of Dallas. It's now known as Texas Woman's University (TWU). Back then, it was the "sister school" of A&M. Girls from TSCW, known as "Tessies," took every opportunity to go to Aggieland. They went to dances and football games with cadets, and my mom was no exception.

She did have one advantage, though. Her father worked for the railroad, so she could ride the train for free. The train I'm talking about took her from her home in Houston to her school in Denton, TX. It always made a stop in College Station (named for the station where the train would stop and let off cadets). She first met my dad on that train, and they played cards most of the trip. When he got off the train in College Station, he almost forgot to ask her name! Luckily, he did ask. So, my mom was as much of an Aggie as she could be!

When I was four years old, my brother left for his first year at A&M. Bill (known to us as Bud) joined the Corps, which by then was optional. He was a member of the national champion Fish Drill Team (a precision rifle team). As most Aggies know, the precision military drill team at the start of the movie *A Few Good Men* is former Fish Drill Team members in Marine Corps uniforms. Bud's performance on that team, and his being an Aggie in general, had a huge impact on my life! I wanted nothing more than to follow in his footsteps as soon as I could. Thirteen years later, I got that chance.

Basically, I was an indoctrinated Aggie from birth. It just got reinforced in new ways every few years.

I spent a lot of time on the campus visiting Bud, especially for Mother's Day weekend (renamed Parents Weekend, and now known as Family

Weekend). My mom was active in the Aggie Moms (a group of women who could truly make things happen), and my dad was an active Former Student.

When it was time for me to choose a school, I applied to the University of Texas, Baylor, and Texas A&M. I eliminated UT because the campus didn't have the "feel" I wanted. I was somewhat torn about Baylor, until I attended the A&M/Baylor football game. I was on the "old Ag" side, **not** with the student body, and I watched the Aggie students participate in a way I hadn't really paid much attention to before. They were a part of something bigger than just a bunch of students. I realized right then that I wanted to be on **that** side of things, with the Aggies. I belonged there.

In the Fall of 1982, I attended Fish Camp, and truly became an Aggie. I started classes in August, living in Keathley Hall with my best friend from high school drill team. We were lucky to get that 4th-floor room, because the dorms filled up quickly. I think my dad knew someone who knew someone because that's how these things used to work.

Thanks to a friend I'd made as a counselor at Camp Arrowhead, I had a date to the first football game with a member of the Fightin' Texas Aggie Band. Back then, the Band was all male, and they could have dates with them in the best seats in Kyle Field. There's no better way to be in the center of the action than to be sitting with "The Pulse of the Spirit of Aggieland."

It's relevant to mention here that when I went to college (especially because it was A&M), I felt like I'd been sent on a mission to find myself an Aggie husband. That would give me value in my parents' eyes for sure. Getting a degree in Journalism was just a happy accident for me.

The academics back then were no challenge for me. I'd skipped a grade at age 10, and was the responsible, compliant, eager student every teacher wanted. However, when I got to college, it was all about getting that "Mrs." degree and enjoying my first taste of freedom. It's an understatement to say I didn't handle it well!

One of the reasons I think I was able to help a lot of students once I got to work more closely with them is that when I was in college, **I made so many mistakes**! I showed a total lack of responsible choices when it came to food, sleep, and schoolwork.

For the first 17 years of my life, my mother oversaw every single decision I made: what I ate, what I wore, where I went, and with whom. I learned to do things because she was watching, not because it was the smart choice. You can imagine, then, how poorly prepared I was to be making those decisions without a real adult around to instruct me. Think how this is somewhat like today's kids having someone take care of everything for them.

The dining hall near our dorm, known as Sbisa (the largest one in the country at the time), was the same place my mom had danced with my dad back in the 1940s. It was also an all-you-can-eat experience once you got in the door. It was all prepaid by my parents, too. They had put aside the money for me to attend college so I could focus and not worry about earning money at a job.

When I lived at home, the only job I could have was babysitting in the neighborhood. No driving to a food service job, or anything like what my brothers were **required** to do.

When I got to college, I was told not to get any kind of job unless it was on campus and directly connected with my academic major. I didn't have a car, anyway, so I wouldn't have been able to get to an off-campus job.

I ended up getting paid to be on the newspaper staff and the yearbook staff, so I did get a little experience and a few dollars of my own. (That time as a student employee even helped with my longevity as a state employee years later!) However, every dollar I earned was put in a checking account monitored by my mom back in Houston.

Food wasn't the only area where I showed my complete lack of self-control. I deliberately stayed up too late, most likely because of a dating-related situation, and slept late. As a freshman, I was put into a lot of 8 a.m. classes. That just wasn't gonna work for me! My motto was "better never than late," so if there was the slightest chance that I'd be late to class, I didn't go.

While my roommate Ingrid attended all her (much harder) classes, and read the textbook in advance, and rewrote her notes, I hardly cracked a book. There were a couple of classes that I hated so much I only went for the first few days and the tests. That would explain the "D" on my grade report. To this day, even though I rarely went to class, I remember the annoying voice of my economics professor (who is still teaching, as Google tells me).

By the time I got to my junior year, I finally figured out how much difference it made to attend class and take notes. It was phenomenal! My classes, of course, became more interesting as I moved into journalism classes instead of "general education." My work on the yearbook and newspaper also made me more interested in learning how to do it well. But don't think for a minute that I gave up on finding that Aggie husband! It was still my #1 priority.

During my sophomore year, I got into a long-term relationship that was headed toward that proposal I craved, and he was the center of my world. As a member of the Aggie Band, he had a group of buddies with whom we did everything. They all had girlfriends, of course, known as "band wives." We had our role, and we played it well (if we wanted to keep the role). All these years later, I think all of them are still married to their Aggie from that group. I didn't marry mine. However, he and I did get married a week apart (to someone else) and were invited to each other's weddings. We're still in touch today.

Looking back, being driven by a desire for freedom and a determination to defy my mother, I wasn't headed for success. I gained the predictable "freshman 15 pounds" and more. I spent money on junk food and other unnecessary things. I deliberately made decisions that would annoy my mom. I squandered an academic opportunity that I didn't fully appreciate at the time. Luckily, I was "brain smart" enough to get a degree in four years without too much struggle. Oh, if only I'd been a different kind of smart.

Now, let's look at the two primary reasons you should hear me out about kids and college. First, we talk more about my daughter Chelsea.

2 kids, 2 paths

Chelsea

When I talked to parents at orientation, I always started my presentation with an explanation of my "credentials." I started with the degrees, and the years in higher education. Then I gave them the **real** credentials: the fact that I'm a mother of two children.

My own mistakes undoubtedly played a role in how I raised my own daughter especially. I'm so pleased to say that she was never as "boy crazy" as I was and didn't seem to connect her personal worth to whether she had a boyfriend. She was confident, outspoken (which can be annoying when they're young but helpful later), and eager to be herself. She knew she had our support and love regardless, and she had the freedom to find her own way.

She was an excellent student from the beginning, and only got in trouble twice. One time for throwing a book at a student who beat her racing into the cafeteria. And once for spitting on a boy in first grade. Even though there was a punishment for that, the principal privately told me that "some kids needed to be spit on." Naturally, that's not the way we wanted her to handle conflict, but at the time, it was amusing.

Chelsea did UIL competitions (storytelling and spelling), played softball, took gymnastics, and made me a soccer mom. She got perfect grades, even if she struggled with tardiness because getting her up in the morning was like waking the dead. I suspect it was because she stayed up reading into the late hours, which was a genetically influenced behavior from both of her parents. The only times, as a child, that she got up early voluntarily were Christmas morning, her birthday, and the day we drove her to sleepaway camp.

She has loved school since the beginning. She is (and was quite early) a voracious reader. She was even good at math, until third grade when long division showed up. But she was responsible, studious, eager, and prepared. I loved seeing how organized she was with everything, partly because it confirmed that I'd passed down some of my good genes.

When choosing a college to attend (there was never a question of whether she'd go to college), she made a pro/con list of her three top schools. One was in Boston (private), the second was the University of North Texas (UNT), and the third was the University of Wyoming (UW). That last one may seem odd, but I was living and working there at the time.

We visited all the schools, and it was entirely her choice. Oh, except for the part where Emerson in Boston was about $40,000 per semester. That's when I told her she was born pretty—not rich. The reason she rejected it wasn't the cost, though. It was the fact that it wasn't a traditional campus like she had grown up with in College Station and too many people were smoking right outside the main building.

So, it was down to UNT and UW. I did everything in my power not to influence her choice. If asked, I provided information, but only what she requested. She loved the new Honors dorm at UNT, because—as my child—she is comfort- and luxury-oriented when it's available. I thought for sure that would get her to enroll in Denton and become part of the "Mean Green."

However, when the time came, I learned through my best friend (and little brother I never had) Dr. Brandon Kosine, in a meeting we were having, that she had chosen Wyoming! I could hardly contain my excitement! I did ask her how much it mattered that I was there, and she finally showed me her pro/con list. The fact that I was in Wyoming was both a pro *and* a con. Go figure.

I later learned that it was in my favor that I had a car she could use, and a kitchen. But the flip side was that I would be close by and she would be compared to me.

The real fun started when she and her dad came to town for her new student conference. I got to move from Area Coordinator mode to Mom mode. Which wasn't all that easy for me! Her dad and I had agreed we'd not hesitate to embarrass her with our questions and hugs, so that was a given.

Where it got tough was when we were in presentations for the parents only, and the presenter was asked a question she wanted a better answer for. The Vice President (the presenter) knew I was in the room and asked me to stand up and answer the question. Oh, how quickly the other parents glommed onto me as a resource! Which, I must admit, was flattering. I truly love to have answers and be helpful.

Naturally, our daughter wouldn't be living in the dorm I supervised. Instead, she was next door, in the tallest occupied building in Wyoming—White Hall. She has a different last name than mine, so not everyone knew right away that she was my daughter. That is, until they saw us together! I had a lot of fun with that her freshman year. I'm not sure how fun it was for her.

Her sophomore year she was hired to be a Resident Advisor. Again—not in my hall. However, she didn't get hired in the first round. She was devastated at that decision and came to my office just crushed. Being my daughter, she was having an emotional melt-down and was convinced she was a complete failure at college. What she didn't know at the time is that I already had been told she was next up if any RAs didn't make grades or accept the offer. Naturally, that happened within days, as I knew it would. It was tough to not be able to comfort her with that information.

Unluckily for her (I think), the entire live-in staff would meet every Monday night for in-service. That put her in a room with about 100 fellow RAs, several professional staff, and her mother. Many times, I was the one on the agenda to present the topic of the week. That had to have made her just a little nervous.

Only once (I think) did I manage to directly embarrass her with my comments, but it wasn't deliberate! It *was*, however, hilarious. I won't repeat it here but suffice it to say it had to do with intimacy. No daughter wants to hear her mom talk about that, especially in front of a bunch of her peers. She has forgiven me, I think.

During Chelsea's junior year in college, Chuck and I decided it was going to be our last year in Wyoming. I would finally be finishing my master's degree, and there was going to be some major change in the department leadership. We were also ready to no longer be living in the dorm.

As much as I loved that job, it provided absolutely zero privacy. It was a three-bedroom, two-bath apartment, but it was across the street from one of the most popular student hangouts. When students would walk by our windows, we could hear every word. When you work for Residence Life, you don't have much of a personal life.

So, I graduated, and we moved back to Texas to be near family. Chelsea went on to be a campus tour guide working at the Admissions office while she finished her degree. She was a student athlete tutor for a semester and lived off campus her senior year. She managed to graduate not only without any debt, but also with money saved.

After she graduated, she moved back to College Station and quickly found a job that was a great fit for her. She ran the front office of the Study Abroad center at Texas A&M. She became an official passport agent and started making a grown-up life for herself.

It didn't take too long for her to decide to go for a master's degree. She chose marketing, not an MBA, after a lot of careful research into what she really wanted to do, and what degree was best for that. Her office arranged to pay her tuition, so once again she had a good plan. She also managed to find scholarships, just as she had—on her own—for undergrad. I was impressed!

When she earned her Aggie Ring in 2017, I was there to hand it to her at the enormous event they now put on for that important Aggie moment. Several thousand students get their rings at each one (I think three times a year). When she graduated not long after, we traveled back from Tennessee to celebrate that as well. I was proud and pleased that she'd done that for herself, including a difficult internship the summer before graduation. That's probably a whole chapter on its own, in another book. However, she never hesitated to ask for help when she needed it, and she made full use of the resources available to her.

She was pretty much a model student, despite her struggle in grad school with an accounting class she had to take (online, while out of the country). It's a different world from when I was in college, and she's a much more confident and focused student.

While it wasn't always easy to be a Student Affairs professional while my daughter was a college student, I think I did learn to keep most of my opinions to myself (unless specifically asked). I never intervened for her with any faculty or staff member. In fact, I could go almost a week without seeing her, and we lived less than 50 yards apart. She did occasionally ask to borrow our car, and sometimes she would do laundry at our apartment. Or ask to come over and bake something.

At no point did she rely on me or use my position to get herself anything on campus. Not that I was that powerful, but I had been there for a few years when she arrived. It wasn't a big place, and someone in my position was continually interacting with others all over campus. So, the connections were there if she wanted them. And people were more than eager to help!

In fact, my husband and I often wondered whether it was just her, or a generational thing, that she resisted the idea we'd both grown up with: it's not *what* you know, it's *who* you know. It pleased me that she didn't bank on my position, but it was also satisfying to be useful from time to time.

Back when Chelsea was in Wyoming, more than once she was called my "mini-me." But she had much more confidence. She had good friends, tried new things, and thoroughly enjoyed living in a place that was so different from where she grew up.

All in all, her educational experience was a parent's dream. Even a normal parent who didn't spend her career on a college campus would have recognized that she fit well into the college environment and made the most of her opportunities. Her father (and stepfather) and I were overjoyed.

Once she found her first professional role after grad school, she moved to Dallas and started really "adulting" full time. I was delighted that she was becoming what she wanted to be and doing so much of it on her own. She did have a steady boyfriend within months of arriving back in Aggieland, but "finding a husband" was never a priority for her. She wanted to truly be moving toward goals that mattered to her. It was so rewarding to see her turn into the young woman I had not been able to be. I wasn't living *through* her, but I was beyond pleased to see her improve on my efforts.

Davis

Meanwhile, her brother Davis was four years behind her in age and in school and was at **least** as intelligent and well-read as she was. Surely, we were in for another positive experience. We had no doubts about how smart he was and how good he was at everything he tried. Music, sports, you name it.

He read every book in the school library and had to go find more. He earned so many Accelerated Reader points that he gave some to friends so they could buy things at the reward store. His teachers all liked him, and he had an adventurous spirit when he visited Wyoming. Sometimes it seemed like he was part mountain goat. He even loved shoveling the snow (of course, he didn't have to, so that probably made it a lot more fun).

By the time he was ready to finish high school, we had moved back to College Station to be near our aging parents, and he moved in with us. The adventures were just beginning, and we were about to realize just how different one child can be from another—and not just in age and gender.

We learned many lessons as Davis went through his teens. We weren't fully prepared for what it would lead us all through, but we were going to be there for him. Little did I know, back then, how much his choices and experiences would shape me as an Academic Coach, and as a mom.

As I said before, I would tell parents during my orientation presentation that they should listen to me for a couple of reasons. Here's how it typically went.

Picture yourself as a parent in your first session without your college student—and it's often your first time having a college student. You have this middle-aged woman up in front, not really needing a microphone, and starting a Power Point presentation on the big screens. I'd describe my official credentials in higher ed, then I'd mention my two kids, like this.

"I have two now-grown 'children,' both of whom went to college right after high school. The oldest, my daughter, finished her bachelor's degree in four years—with no summer school—and will soon finish a master's degree.

My son, her younger brother, well… (*insert long pause for effect*) he left after one semester with 4 W grades (withdraw) and an F. But he made **great** friends at the local hookah bar!" Okay, it was also a coffee shop, but that doesn't sound as funny.

After the laughter died down, I'd go on to explain that they're both highly intelligent, interesting individuals who were raised in a college town—literally lived in a college dorm before age 10. I'd tell the group that one was ready, and the other wasn't. One we tried hard to keep up with, and the other we pushed. Way too hard. It quickly became painfully apparent how much college didn't fit my son at age 18. His dad and I really wanted him to attend college, and knew he was more than smart enough. His grandparents had provided him with enough money to go to school as well, so that wasn't an issue.

Unfortunately, he only went to college because we expected it of him and his girlfriend at the time was going. He chose the same college she did, about 50 miles from their hometown.

I got to be the one to go to his orientation sessions, and we had a good time. He asked good questions at the sessions and seemed eager to get started. He even signed up to play a couple of sports. His father got to take him on move-in day and told me it all went well.

What started as a positive thing didn't last.

Before long, he was no longer going to class. He wasn't participating in sports and was rarely seen in his dorm. I still don't know what he was doing that semester—and I'm not sure I'll ever really want to know all of it. But he has made it clear that he just didn't get into the whole student thing. It wasn't the right time or place for him, and that became obvious to him quickly.

Not so much to us.

We would ask the typical questions a parent is expected to ask and get the usual non-committal and vague answers. We didn't want to push much more, though, because we were just glad he was going to school.

Why would it surprise us that he was going to school? After all, he was smart and did finish high school.

Sort of.

He had been late so many times and skipped so many classes that we got a call from one of the principals at his huge high school telling us that he wasn't going to graduate. He just didn't have the credits or attendance, and the only option at this point was to do a "special" program where he would try to finish the classes online in a computer lab, supervised by a teacher.

Well, he didn't want to stay in high school, that's for sure. And I believe we'd already ordered the cap and gown and invitations for graduation. So, he agreed to go to the computer lab and see what he could do to complete a semester.

He was done in less than three days, finishing work normally done in about half a semester. We were so relieved that he'd be graduating! Turns out, they have their own ceremony for that program, so he wouldn't be attending the one for his regular high school. Frankly, he didn't really care about missing it. However, I had already planned a college graduation trip with my daughter to California, and we had planned it around the *normal* high school graduation date. We couldn't really change the trip, and he said he didn't care who was at whatever graduation he had to attend.

His dad and his stepdad attended his special ceremony together. Imagine their surprise when they didn't call my son's name, and he didn't appear at any point in the ceremony. His dad received a text about that time from my son. It said Davis would be missing his own graduation because he had a meeting that he couldn't skip with his probation officer.

Oh, I didn't mention that part of his earlier high school adventures?

Imagine my surprise when, on a bright and early football Saturday in College Station, home of Texas A&M and host to an obscene number of visitors on that weekend, I received a call from a bail bondsman. This bail bondsman told me that I needed to come bail my son out of jail. I said, "You must be mistaken—my son is asleep in his room." She encouraged me to go check on that.

So, I walked down the hall to his room, knocked on the door, and received no answer. That wasn't entirely unusual, as he was a dedicated sleeper, so I knocked again then opened the door. You guessed it—he wasn't there. I went back to the phone and asked the bail bondsman how much it would cost to get him out, and when I needed to be there.

I woke my husband up and told him what was going on and let him know that I would be getting dressed and going to Bryan to bail Davis out of jail. He was quite comforting to me, said all the right things, and offered to go with me. I declined, although I was so grateful for his continuing support. It wasn't the first time we'd had a call about Davis's choices, but it was the first one that involved actual jail. The others had just been smoking cigarettes on the high school campus—twice in two weeks—and the ticket and penalties that came with getting caught.

When I got downtown, where all the bail bonds offices were that I never expected to visit, I learned a bit more about what had happened and how long I'd be waiting for Davis. I paid and listened to them tell me he'd been arrested at a parking garage with his girlfriend, smoking pot. Great.

Later, when I finally got Davis into the car, he was just crushed and obviously tired and upset. He finally had his cell phone back and called his girlfriend (whose parents had bailed her out the night before—her dad worked for the women's prison), then called his dad. He gave me a little explanation for what had happened, including the climbing out the window to get into his girlfriend's car to go smoke weed.

His arrest and trip to jail in the police car sounded rough, but at this point I was surprised I could even speak to him. I was shocked, hurt, afraid, and unable to be much good to anyone—especially to my son who had just crossed a line. Driving back to our house across town, I made it clear to him that he'd be going to his job at Sonic that day, regardless of how much sleep he didn't get in the jail cell.

We worked our way through the legal process over the coming weeks, and he got a chance to redeem himself with probation and community service. That's why he wasn't at his graduation ceremony. It just seemed like a cherry on top of a non-traditional way of finishing public school. Keep in mind that I found out about his non-attendance at that ceremony from my husband, who called me in California to let me know what had happened. That just gave me more to look forward to discussing with Davis when I returned, especially on the topic of two-way communication with one's parents.

I guess by the time he was headed off to Sam Houston State (in Huntsville TX, where the infamous "death row" prison is), I thought he might have figured out that college could be his ticket to a better future. He chose psychology as his major, because he's always been fascinated by human behavior. He's a great writer, too, but just doesn't enjoy doing it.

Did I mention that he's always been extra smart, good at everything he tries, and the kind of student the teachers liked? And as I introduced him to a former colleague of mine at his new school, and I saw his great attitude about everything, I had such high hopes.

Little did I know he was showing me and telling me what I so desperately wanted to hear. He knew exactly how to play it. And I had learned enough about helicopter parenting that I was determined **not** to be one. I wasn't going to call him and check up on him. I wasn't going to visit unless invited. I had joined the parent group for Sam Houston and was ready to be all kinds of supportive—on request.

As we learned later from Davis, there really wasn't anything his dad or I could have done to make that college experience come out right. He wasn't ready, it wasn't a good fit, and he was determined to make the most of a total lack of supervision.

Even though his dad and I hadn't been overly protective and restrictive the way I was raised, we may have trusted him a bit too much—or not enough.

He has since told me that he was bound and determined at that point to do "whatever the hell he wanted to do," regardless of what was best. It shouldn't have come as that much of a surprise to me, since I knew that feeling. But I guess it did surprise me because I knew he'd been raised differently than I had. Didn't that mean he'd make better choices? Apparently not.

Granted, he was four years old when his dad and I split up, so that probably had some impact. I moved to Wyoming when he was eleven, and his dad was left to handle most things by himself. Mike is/was a great dad, but we were both being fooled by the time Davis was a teenager.

Davis did tell me, on one of his visits to the mountains, that he had tried pot and "please don't tell Dad." I agreed not to tell, hoping he would continue to trust me with more details about his life. I did encourage him to tell his dad on his own, but he was afraid of how his dad would react. After all, his dad had never done drugs (nor had I) and had never been an alcohol drinker (I can't claim that). His dad is just an overall good guy. Davis just didn't want his dad to see the reality of what was going on when he wasn't watching.

Davis told me that the divorce and my departure didn't force him to make those choices. He continues to not understand how, as his parents, we naturally questioned our parenting when we found out what was going on. He insists it was all on him. He says we had set good examples and given him a good amount of freedom—not too little or too much. He was just too good at deceiving us and too determined to do whatever he could get away with. I'm still not sure I believe it, and maybe his story will change if/when he has teenagers of his own.

Meanwhile, he had some ups and downs since leaving college after one semester. He tried working—at Sonic restaurant, at McAllister's Deli, at a car wash, grilling steak at Freebird's World Burrito, and mowing lawns. He was a hard worker and had incredibly high standards at each job (as he still does).

For example, when things were slow on a shift at Sonic, Davis would look for work to do—no matter how menial. He would clean bathrooms, re-stock cups, or do whatever else needed to be done. Meanwhile, his fellow carhops were hovering at the front, waiting to get the next customer and hope for tips.

Those employment situations worked for a while, as did his volatile relationship with the above-mentioned girlfriend. He even moved out of his dad's house for a while and lived with her. He later tried having a few roommates at his dad's house after his dad remarried and moved into another house with his new wife. Things were unraveling, though, and he needed a change.

We had moved to Nashville to be near grandchildren in 2015, after three years back in College Station. Davis wasn't living with us when we moved, but a year later he called and asked if he could come live with us. He needed a fresh start and he had liked Tennessee when he visited.

At age 21, he drove all the way here in one night and arrived exhausted in August 2016. Just a few days later, with a referral from dear friend Jane who was an exec with Texas Roadhouse, he earned a job as a grill cook at our local restaurant. Slowly he managed to get things together and enjoyed earning money for his high-quality work at Roadhouse.

We enjoyed seeing him cook those steaks—and loved our family discount! He seemed to be happier and was little-by-little severing ties with the girlfriend back in Texas.

At the time, I was a success coach at the local community college, and I could get him a great rate to attend if he wanted. He knew the life he wanted would most likely require a degree, and he thought he was ready to try again. We got him enrolled at the last minute, thanks to generous and helpful coworkers of mine, and it seemed like it would finally come together.

Once again, we didn't realize how much we pushed him into it, and how much of it was our idea—not his. He still wasn't ready, and we didn't see it. Looks like young people aren't the only ones who can be slow learners.

He left college again and continued to work a late-night and all-weekend schedule at Texas Roadhouse, coming home exhausted and sleeping the next morning until it was time to go to work again. He made some friends at work, which was a great thing in our eyes. There was even an older married bartender there who said she'd keep an eye on him for me.

It was after a long double shift at Roadhouse that Davis was driving home one Sunday night. He had really been pulling his life together, and he said he had so much hope for his future.

Driving home that Memorial Day weekend around midnight, he came upon a check point of police cars about a mile from our house. He realized that he had a small bag of weed in the glove box of the truck and panicked. He could just see all his steps forward being wiped away by an arrest. So, instead of stopping and hoping they wouldn't ask to see anything in the truck, he floored it. Hit 70 miles per hour in a 45 zone and ended up being chased by three cars to the front of our house.

I was in bed at this point, and my husband came to wake me up, saying, "You'd better get your wits about you and put on a robe." Naturally, I asked why. "Because Davis is handcuffed in the back of the Sheriff's car in front of our house."

I was beyond stunned. I couldn't speak. Thankfully, my husband could. He went outside to see what all was going on, and Davis looked at him and said, "Well, I guess I'll see you guys in a few weeks." Why a few weeks? Well, we were planning to get on a plane in a day or two to fly overseas for our first trip to the UK.

The Sheriff let him know he'd probably make bail and be out in the morning. They impounded the truck, and took Davis in. He asked Chuck to find the cash he'd been helping him save for emergencies and bring it to bail him out the next day. Chuck agreed to do that, and we picked him up shortly before noon.

I asked Davis what time he had to be at work, and he said he didn't get any sleep in the jail cell. I said, "You're going to work—you need the money now more than ever."

He did go to work that day, and when we saw him awake again, he asked for a referral to an attorney. We connected him with a good friend from church who knows everyone around here, and they talked. Davis was referred to a fantastic attorney and handled everything himself from that point on. He didn't ask for another dime, didn't ask us to attend any meetings with the attorney, and didn't ask us to join him in court. He said it was **his** huge mistake, and he was going to take care of it.

After a while, he realized he wanted to earn more money, so he took on an additional job working days with a local high-end landscaping company. He was referred by one of the other "grill guys" at Roadhouse who also worked in landscaping, and Davis was eager to spend more time outside (especially since it wasn't in the Texas heat that he remembered). That lasted until he went 70 days straight without any time off, and he just couldn't do both jobs anymore.

He now works full time (and more) just for the landscaping company and loves the work. He loves what he's learning and has incredibly high standards for his work. Just as he became what we called a "steak snob" when he was grilling them, he has become a landscaping snob. Luckily, we benefit from both on occasion.

Has he abandoned the idea of college? Not entirely. He still has an interest in computers and has investigated a degree in Cyber Security. Our local community college has a good program, and he could finish the degree in under two years (at the pace he learns and considering how much of it is online). At age 24 and financially emancipated, he'd even qualify for Tennessee Reconnect.

But I've told him that I won't mention it again. I'll never again tell him when or where or how to get an education if he wants one. I won't try to tell him how to spend his work life, or whom to choose as a spouse (if he decides to choose one). But if he ever asks for my advice, I'm here. He knows that and says he values it. I'll have to just trust that he'll use it when the time comes. Clearly, my previous approach wasn't ever going to work.

How much of it was his personality? How much was rebellion? Was it depression or anxiety? We may never know. We just know he's not his sister or his parents. He's a smart, hard-working, talented, witty, energetic, lovable young man. He still voluntarily initiates hugs in public with his mother. He tells anyone he knows who's in college (or considering a career change) how much his mom can help with all of that. He calls and texts us and requests that we get together for meals or to just hang out. He offers to cook steaks for us and seems to truly enjoy our company.

Whether he gets a college degree or not, he won't be a failure in my eyes. If he uses his God-given skills, abilities, and talents to do something useful, legal, and interesting (to him), I'm happy. I just hope I get to share in his life and see how it develops.

My professional experience

Back in the summer of 2000, right after I married Chuck, I was hired to supervise a staff of eight student Resident Advisors, who were hired by someone else a few months before. Oddly enough, I was hired to lead this staff in the hall I'd lived in back in my senior year at Texas A&M. As it was back then (1985-86), Krueger Hall was all female, and mostly filled with freshmen (what we now call first-year students). It was four floors, without elevators, made up of suite-style rooms. That meant there were two female students in a room, connected by a bathroom to another room with two more female students. I'm still friends with one of my suitemates from way back then, the amazing Jodi Savoie Eubanks, and have some good memories of my time in Krueger.

Strangely enough, even though I had lived in campus housing all four years of my undergraduate time at A&M, I had no idea there were full-time professionals getting paid to live in the dorm. I did get a laugh when I remembered the reason my parents told me I couldn't move to an apartment while I was in college. They said, "This is the only time in your life you can live in a dorm—you can live in an apartment any time!" No matter the age, we still get a bit of satisfaction when our parents are "wrong" about something!

I knew there were RAs, and I knew there was some kind of "hall council" because I had done the newsletter for my dorm during my first two years. But I really didn't remember seeing a "professional" around the dorm. My first ResLife boss, Rick Turnbough, confirmed for me that there was indeed a Hall Director back then because he knew her by name: Cindy. He could even show me where she'd lived.

At this point in 2000, I was wondering quite a few things:
- If I didn't remember my own Hall Director, how could I hope to make an impact?
- How would being a mom fit into this role?
- How could I be a good supervisor for eight young people I'd never met?
- How could I be a good supervisor at all, having never been one?
- What would it be like to live in a dorm again, after living in the suburbs for a decade?

These questions would all be answered for me quickly, although the answer for a couple of them would change more than once. But first, let me back up to how I even found out about this job.

One of my many roles on the Texas A&M campus was as the communications office (all by myself) for the HR Department, as I mentioned earlier. I started this position when I was expecting my first child in 1991. I worked at HR for about three years, making some life-long friends and professional contacts I value to this day.

A few years and a few jobs later, my marriage was dissolving (as I mentioned earlier). I was dissatisfied with my career, and things just had to change. I quit my job, moved a few miles away into an apartment (leaving the kids with their wonderful dad), and joined Coach University to learn how to be a personal success coach. Shortly after all this happened, I also met the man I'm still married to.

After about a year in Coach U, I was discovering that phone-based coaching wasn't appealing to me. I was much more about being in the same room with someone who needed me. At the time, Skype didn't exist, and video conferencing wasn't common or free in any form I knew of.

This is where a fateful contact came from Susan Causey whom I worked with at that original HR job. She "tricked" me into becoming a good public speaker (that's another story for another time), and told me, "You ought to wait and have your daughter on **my** birthday—not the July 4th due date!"

I've mostly forgiven Susan for that birthday thing (which **did** happen the way she requested) because of the speaking thing and the next thing I'll describe.

She knew that I was doing the Coach U training, had two kids (her daughter was one of our best babysitters) and my marriage had ended. She contacted me to tell me about a job opening on the A&M campus that she thought would be perfect for me.

I'd never heard of it before.

She said to use her as a reference and I was aware that she knew everyone, and they all loved and respected her. I read the job description for the Hall Director position, and realized it was exactly what I'd been looking for. It would allow me to do so much of what I'd wanted to do, and in a role that I didn't know had a salary (and a living space) attached to it.

While planning my wedding with Chuck, scheduled for June 10, I applied for the job and got an interview. It was a fun interview—much more intense than any I'd done before—and I left knowing it was where I wanted to be. I also left to get married and go on a honeymoon that included Chuck interviewing for a position in College Station (he had been living about eight hours away). After our brief honeymoon, we both got calls saying we got the jobs. So, it was meant to be!

To be clear, this isn't a job I could have even considered if I had still been married to my first husband. Not because he wasn't supportive, but because it wouldn't have fit our life. Nonetheless, he was supportive of this change, and we continued to have a good, strong, coparent relationship when I lived in Krueger Hall. My kids had an amazing set of experiences they wouldn't otherwise have had, and I'm convinced that being a parent made me a better Hall Director and vice versa.

I give you this lengthy glimpse at my professional background, especially in the dorms, so you'll know I took a non-traditional path to what I've learned about college students.

I worked on a college campus in some capacity from 1987 to 2018, but it wasn't until the Hall Director position in 2000 that I truly got a chance to interact with students both one-on-one and in groups. I got to spend time with some student leaders and some lost young people. I was exposed to parenting behavior that greatly shaped my own—both as great examples and as dire warnings.

The transition into a live-in position changed my life forever. It has shaped me as a woman, a professional, a parent, an educator, and a friend. And now, it's led me to write my first book.

Residence Life

After all the lead-in I've provided, it's time to tell you more about the strange (and wonderful) dorm job I had.

As I mentioned earlier, people are usually surprised when they hear that I used to be a "dorm mom." Some of them are like me and didn't realize when they lived in a dorm way back when that there was someone paid to "run" the dorm. Most of them knew about the RA, but few knew who supervised them. Others are just amazed that anyone (especially my age) would voluntarily live in a dorm for a job.

It helps a little when I explain that we had an apartment on the first floor—not a standard dorm room. At Texas A&M, it was a pretty small apartment. One bedroom, one bath, a living room, two closets, and a kitchenette (less than 700 square feet total). We used to joke that the oven was an Easy Bake that used only a large light bulb.

The apartment was just inside the main entrance to the dorm, and right across from the stairs. This building was only four stories tall, so it didn't have elevators. You can imagine the panic that caused on a hot August move-in day! In fact, that leads me to one of my husband's favorite stories from our days in Krueger Hall. Trust me, it's relevant.

One hot August day, which in central Texas can be in the triple digits, I heard a knock on my open apartment door. It was the weekend, so Chuck was home. I had just stopped in for something during the cat-herding of move-in day, so someone must have told these people where to find me.

It was a mother and her daughter, and the daughter was in tears. I quickly introduced myself and asked how I could help. The mother spoke up, saying, "We have a problem with my daughter's room."

Naturally, I asked what the problem was. She answered, "It's on the 4th floor." I stopped myself from laughing and, instead, said, "So, what's the problem?" At this point, the sobbing student cried out, "It's just so *far*!" The mom chimed in with, "Can you just move her down a few floors, so she doesn't have to do so much walking and climbing the stairs?"

I could hear Chuck's snort of laughter-turned-into-a-cough in the kitchenette, and somehow, I managed to keep my composure. I told them that even if I wanted to move her down a few floors, I couldn't, because our dorm was 100% full. There were no openings on **any** floor. I also gently pointed out that classes were held all over our enormous campus, so walking would become a habit for her (or riding a bike).

Our building was right next to a bus stop, which would be helpful, but the campus is literally one of the largest physical plants in the country. (A physical plant in the world of college campuses is the land and buildings on that land that make up the campus, even if it's divided by roads or railroad tracks.) She left my office disappointed and sad, but perhaps with a small dose of reality.

After they were gone, Chuck joined me in the living room and said, "Wow—I thought you were going to lose it! Do you think she expects her professors to come to her room to teach? Do you think she's planning to have her meals delivered?" We just cracked up about that, even while being appalled that the 4th floor was such an issue to this young lady.

By the way, she didn't have any *visible* indications of a reason why she couldn't climb four flights of stairs. She seemed healthy and able. Had that not been the case, she would have been accommodated from the start with a room designed to make her life easier. We do that all the time. But there was no apparent reason for her to need a first-floor room. None. How I wish I'd kept up with her, to see if she stayed, and if she learned just how different life was about to be.

Okay, back to my ResLife (as opposed to a normal life).

My office was crawling distance from our apartment's one-and-only door, so my commute was no problem! That matters a lot in the middle of the night when most things go wrong on a college campus. It also impacted my selection of pajamas. Much to my husband's disappointment, I had relatively good taste in PJs, and bought plenty to prove it. I mean, if you're going to be dealing with the campus police and drunk students, you probably ought to look somewhat presentable, even if it's 2 a.m.

My office was a converted dorm suite where they took out the wall between the bedrooms. They left the connecting bathroom, and just emptied the room of the normal dorm furniture. It was truly a large office! We managed to fit a comfortable sectional couch on one side—the side that also had my work desk. On the other side was a nice bunk bed set for my kids, as well as another sofa and some storage for their things. It was a pretty good set-up!

It was good, but strange. There was no dividing wall between the kids' "bedroom" space and the office. Then again, way too often, my kids just fell asleep on the couch in the main apartment watching TV or a movie (cable was provided in the dorm).

I shared that office with the student staff who were my RAs. Because this was an all-female dorm, my staff was also female. I had not selected them—all sophomores and above—because I wasn't working there the previous spring when they were hired. I have to say my predecessor did a great job, for the most part. Only one of them ended up hiding a kitten. In her no-pets-allowed room. That was discovered by a campus administrator taking a tour of our dorm's facilities with me. That "meow" was tough to explain.

I'm hoping this description gives you a little insight into the unusual nature of the job. I was technically living and working in the same building, but the word "work" was completely redefined for me. It seemed to me that the RA staff did the hard stuff. They lived on opposite ends of each floor and had a roommate and suitemates who didn't help with the job. Sometimes, they made it even harder!

My staff wasn't technically "on duty" 24/7, but it could certainly feel that way. Any time they were in the dorm, they could be asked a question or told about a maintenance issue or complained to about a roommate. They had to learn quickly how to set appropriate boundaries because some of the students could be incredibly self-centered and demanding. Others could be sweet and wonderful and make the job a real pleasure.

Before I go further, here's a way-too-brief and over-simplified job description for an RA.

Resident Assistants help students get situated to life in a university residence hall and enhance their on-campus experience, both academic and outside the classroom. They assist fellow residents with personal and educational matters while fostering a sense of community with all residents. Resident Assistants do this by planning activities, providing up-to-date and helpful information on bulletin boards, and keeping a safe environment for all students under their watch. They attend staff meetings, have on-duty shifts, and assist with emergencies related to students and to the building.

They do all this while being full-time students themselves. Some get paid a small stipend and some get free room and board. It depends on the school how they're compensated.

I'll describe what I mean by "self-centered and demanding" mentioned above with this story.

January 17, 2002, during my second year in Krueger Hall, my brother Bud died from metastatic melanoma. He had only been diagnosed six months earlier, and it was too late at that point to save him. On that horrible day, I had just received a phone call from my sister-in-law Eileen that Bud had just died. We knew it was coming, but of course I wasn't ready. I had planned a "goodbye" phone call with him for that morning, but he just didn't make it.

After hanging up from talking with Eileen, I opened my apartment door to head to my office so I could notify my staff and supervisors. As soon as I opened the door, a student coming down the stairs saw me and said, "Oh good—I need to talk to you!" It was clear that I'd been crying, but I said to her, "I just found out that my brother died, so this isn't really a good time to talk." She huffed, put her hands on her hips, and said, "Well, then who's going to get the AC fixed in my room? It's *too hot*!"

As stunned as I was, and as much as it hurt, I said to her, "Okay, follow me to the office and I'll get your name and room number so someone can take care of it." Apparently, that satisfied her, but it made me want to quit on the spot.

Meanwhile, my boss Rick had put a white rose outside my door with a note to honor my brother (I still have it). He and his boss Sue Foster made the 100-mile drive to attend Bud's funeral, too. The support was incredible.

Keep in mind that this dorm, built in 1972, was home-away-from-home for 460 mostly first-year female students. I'm not sure it's *ever* a good idea to have that many women living in one place—and I developed this opinion during my two years in that dorm. Too many young women living in one place was a hormonal nightmare. Just like the same number of guys in the same place is a recipe for horrible smell and disgusting mess.

For some reason (that someone else has probably researched), co-ed dorms are better (in my opinion). The only place we still currently separate by gender to this extreme is prison.

Most schools these days have moved to single-gender floors or sections or suites. Not entire buildings. Some schools have made everything mixed gender, including bathrooms. That's much more progressive than I've seen, but I know it's being done.

What I learned about the boy/girl behavior in a mixed-gender dorm is that the boys tend to be less disgusting, and the girls tend to be less "catty." Maybe they're showing off for each other? I don't know. But I do know that after Krueger, I swore I'd never again live in an all-female hall.

Luckily, my next work assignment was in a co-ed building, Lechner Hall. It had males on the first and third floors, and females on second and fourth. It also helped that the hall was made up entirely of first-year Honors students who were on some sort of competitive academic scholarship. They had a lot more to lose if there was trouble, although when they did cause trouble, it was incredibly creative. Who knew that's what happened to CDs in a microwave?

That dorm also had a group of specially selected sophomores who had lived there the year before as freshmen and competed to get a slot as a sophomore advisor (SA). They lived in pairs on each floor and were led by one junior advisor (JA) who was chosen from the previous SA group.

They were volunteers, and still had to pay room rent. They were completely dedicated to giving the first-year students an amazing experience at A&M, and they did it well. So, you might say that dorm mom job was a bit easier. It also didn't hurt that the building was one of the newest on campus (at the time), and our apartment reflected that. The entire facility benefited from the generosity of the Honors Program, so it was an exceptional environment.

Out to the Mountain West

Things developed in my career even further when I had the opportunity to move to the University of Wyoming in 2006.

Moving to Laramie, Wyoming, home of the only four-year school in the state, was a dramatic change. It was somewhat unexpected, too, as I had once vowed never to live outside of Texas.

Why? Because a few years earlier, I had found myself on a mountain in a minivan that was about to slide off a cliff. I just *knew* I wasn't qualified or brave enough to ever go somewhere like that again, so as I prayed to not be killed that afternoon, I also decided to stay where I was more comfortable, in flat central Texas.

By the way, this moment of panic and resolution was on the way to the Colorado wedding of one of my RA staff. Her soon-to-be father-in-law had to rescue our van, which no longer had a rear windshield. Did I mention this was December, and it was day two of a 12-day vacation?

You can see why my decision to move to Wyoming was somewhat startling. My husband and I did our research, and decided that, for our safety and my sanity, we wouldn't do anything *deliberately* stupid once we moved there. We'd ask for advice from the locals and follow it. I still have the list of what you need in your car emergency kit at least seven months of the year when living in Wyoming. It's a different world!

When people came to visit us, they would ask what those railroad crossing arms were that they could see on the highway. There's no train, so why the crossing arms? It was fun to explain that those were used to close the roads when they became unsafe to travel. They weren't a suggestion—the roads were **closed**. The penalty for driving past them was enormous. I'd call it an idiot tax, if they survived the foolishness of making that decision.

I experienced firsthand being the last car on the road when the arms went down behind me. I wish they'd closed it sooner! Driving in a sideways blizzard is no fun. Almost being hit by an 18-wheeler as you do a 360-degree spin on a bridge covered in ice is a terrifying experience. God was looking after me even more closely that evening.

When I wasn't on snow-blown roads in Wyoming, I had an amazing apartment to live in on campus. It was in Downey Hall (ironically Downey was previous last name, and the one my kids both have), which was built the year I was born. It was made up **tons** of locally quarried stone! The apartment, which had a patio, was a three-bedroom, two-bath *palace* compared to previous living arrangements.

We had a real kitchen, even if there was no dishwasher (other than my husband). Ironically, at this school we didn't *need* the kitchen. The dining hall was award-winning, connected to my building by a well-lit tunnel, and provided us with free meals as part of my compensation. We were living the dream!

That dream was happening on the first floor of an eight-story building on a beautiful wooded campus. My office, with a wall of windows looking outside, felt like it was in a Christmas tree farm. Especially when the huge flakes of snow would start to fall—in almost any month of the year. My office also had a buffer—a locked front desk area staffed by RAs. That's where the students could get mail, borrow a vacuum (for when mom is on the way to visit), and ask questions. Nobody could get into my office without going through them. And they were quite good at being gatekeepers.

Of course, they were also good at pranks—such as embedding all my desk supplies in Jell-O. The person in charge of that prank is now in a very responsible position on a college campus—and is more than qualified. I'm sure karma will catch up with him at some point. If it hasn't yet, it will, Corey!

For one year, while Downey Hall was undergoing a massive renovation, I lived and worked next door in White Hall. It just happens to be the tallest occupied building in Wyoming.

Remember—this is the least populated state in the United States. When you're on the 12th floor of White Hall, and it's exceptionally windy, you can feel it sway a bit. It's also at the corner of one of the busiest streets in the state. In that dorm, I had 22 student staff members, and I also got to supervise a former frat house that had been renovated into a very nice Honors House. All this time, I was also the Advisor for the Residence Hall Association (RHA). That's a student-led group trying to represent the needs of all residents and make the campus living experience the best it can be.

Working with those young people was an experience that again transformed my life.

Some had so much to learn and were making mistakes at a rapid pace. More than once, they ended up losing their jobs because of it. But one of those RAs also thanked me for the wake-up call she got by getting fired. She took me to lunch later and told me how it made her realize where she was making huge mistakes and forced her to fix them. She went on to do good things at UW.

As Chuck and I said to each other all the time, "They're here to learn."

Of course, I learned from them as well.

When I was their age, I didn't have the nerve or self-confidence to be a leader on campus. I didn't even apply to be an RA or serve on hall council. The most I did was a newsletter for my dorm because the RA asked me to. Oh, and I was on judicial board (a student disciplinary board) because someone else quit and I happened to be at the wrong place at the wrong time. I didn't enjoy that role as a student, and I didn't really enjoy it all that much as a professional.

Although the disciplinary meetings weren't my favorite part of running a residence hall, sometimes a relationship could come out of them, and some learning took place.

Sometimes it seemed like I only got to meet the cream-of-the-crop student leaders, the employees, or the people in trouble. The average student didn't really *need* to see me! Not that I wasn't available to them—they just weren't my typical constituents. Again, that's where my student staff took on the bulk of the work. They were the ones "walking rounds" each night, and working the front desk, and putting on programs, and taking on maintenance issues. They didn't get paid much, but there were some benefits to the job.

In fact, I developed a workshop for them so they'd all understand how the RA experience could be useful no matter what kind of career they were planning to pursue. It's even useful if you want to be a stay-at-home parent! It was so gratifying to see, as we worked our way through the material at in-service those nights, just how many transferable skills they had gathered in the job. They had never looked at it that way.

A good RA learns so many things that any employer should value. Communication skills, problem solving, incident reporting, listening, group development, organization, life planning, customer service, and more. The students I've kept in touch with (and there are many), have all been able to say how their residence life experience helped them. It still comes up in conversation when we get together, when we post a memory on Facebook, or when I get a chance to be a job reference (which has happened more than I ever expected).

The experience has shaped me, too. In my campus jobs since leaving residence life—both of which were academic success coaching jobs—I've met many colleagues who were also in Res Life. We have an instant connection and understanding that you had to experience to truly get.

We interacted with just about every office on our campus at some point and *lived with* our primary purpose for being—the students. We dealt with them at all hours and in all situations. We didn't go home at night and separate from campus life. It made up the bulk of our life.

When I was "on call" as a dorm director, I carried a cell phone that had to be on and ready 24/7 for a week, several times each semester. That included not leaving the city limits (in Laramie), and not leaving campus at night (at A&M).

It also included a promise to consume no alcoholic beverages the entire duty cycle. Talk about a time when you felt like you could really use a glass of wine!

And the phone usually rang after 2 a.m. That's just the way it was.

At UW, there weren't "visitation hours" so the calls weren't like those at A&M, when a boy was discovered in a girl's room after a certain time. At UW, calls usually involved an injury, an intoxication of some kind, or a hospital transport. We learned quickly that any time you accompanied a student to the ER, you were there for a minimum of six hours.

We got to know the police well, and almost all of them had our backs and appreciated what we did and where we lived. Only one that I remember had a sort of "bad ass" attitude and treated us like ignorant underlings. We did get to watch him flex and hear him yell. That was a treat.

One of the saddest parts of our job was trying to help suicidal residents. It seems like coping skills are missing in way too many young people these days. And it seems like too many are either unwilling or unable to ask for help from those who are there, and trained, to do just that.

I've been through countless hours of suicide prevention training and even became train-the-trainer certified. Especially in Wyoming, it was a real issue.

I had an RA tell me this story, and it perfectly illustrates what was asked of the live-in staff.

> *Normally I would have gone to class already, but for some reason I was running late. I was about to leave when someone knocked on my door. It was one of my residents, a female, and she was in tears. She told me she had just swallowed a bottle of pills because she wanted to die, but she had reconsidered. She didn't know what to do. I stayed with her and dialed 9-1-1 and made sure she got the medical and mental health care she needed. It scares me to think of what might have happened if I'd been gone. She didn't know that many people in the hall after only being there a couple of months, and most people had gone to class already. I'll never forget that.*

As Sue Foster said in the speech that she sent me, we get trained to approach students who may be suicidal, but we're never completely comfortable with it. She couldn't even recall how many times she asked a student the critical question, "Are you thinking about killing yourself?" She concluded that part of her speech by saying, "College isn't a haven from everyday realities—it's a city unto itself, and there is serious stuff that goes on."

The former head of the Counseling Center at Texas A&M once told me that every time a student answers "Yes" to that question, it still scares her. This is a trained doctor who works with college students for a living. It's still not *ever* what you want to hear. But the question must be asked.

As much as I loved the job as a live-in professional, after 11 years of trading having a life for having a Res Life, I was ready to live in a personal home again. Chuck and I were both ready for some privacy, some control over my work hours, and the ability to decide what our living quarters looked like.

I admit we had little to complain about in the renovated Downey Hall for our final year, though. We even had a dishwasher, and washer and dryer *in the apartment!* No more going to the basement when the custodial staff wasn't on duty so we could share their washer and dryer. Although we'd been spoiled by the dining hall (I'm not kidding—it was remarkable), we were ready to have a full-sized kitchen where we could cook and have people over.

Thinking of Washakie Dining Center reminds me that the students used to text each other when certain desserts were being served. Brownie pudding was famous and disappeared fast! When we took visiting friends and family to eat there, they were stunned. Named for Native American Chief Washakie (whose grandson was in some of my counseling master's classes), this dining center was truly a treat. We even had a Mongolian-style grill station, and one of the cooks would give me a ton of extra shrimp! My friend Jane lovingly still calls it "The Amazing Chief Buffet," and she's in the restaurant business.

Our apartment in the dorm had been the scene of many staff meetings, Thanksgiving gatherings for those who couldn't go home, game nights, cookie baking, and tearful come-to-Jesus conversations.

It had also been the scene of a Christmas Day waterfall coming in over our patio door after a major freeze and thaw. Which, by the way, was fixed that day by the dedicated maintenance staff.

It was where students knew they could find me at almost any hour of the day or night. Its windows looked out at Business Interstate 80, and the favorite student bar was stumbling distance from our back door. The noise traveled better than many of the patrons.

It was an adventure living in the heart of a college campus, in the middle of a town defined by the university. This may have been like College Station and A&M, but only to a point.

Laramie was a place where Walmart had the best view of the sunset. Where a full football stadium (31,000) made Laramie the second largest town in Wyoming for a few hours. A place where the July 4th parade once had to be canceled because of snow. A place infamous for the tragic death of Matthew Shepard in 1998, and the movies and trials that revisited that horrible event. In fact, when I told a friend from college who's gay that we were moving to Laramie in 2006, he said, "Isn't that the place where they kill people like me?"

Laramie is an unusual place in so many ways, and it was the perfect place to spend six years finishing my master's degree, learning how to be an advisor, meeting people who grew up in the mountain west, and trying my first snowshoes.

The connections we made there are precious, and the memories are often indescribable (as much as I try). We had fun. We laughed a lot, and sometimes we cried. Those tears were often of frustration or, at other times, sadness over the choice a student had made. We rolled our eyes a lot at the behavior of the students, and we did our best to remember that they were just kids, really.

I remember discovering that on opening day, one of my non-married colleagues would wear a wedding ring so the parents would think she was older and more responsible. It was hard to argue with that, having been told by parents how much better they felt when they saw me and my husband in the lobby near the front desk and our apartment. They felt like their children were in good hands, even though I made it clear we didn't do bed checks.

Which reminds me of something I told parents who were in a panic over co-ed dorms.

I hated to burst their bubble, but they needed to understand that if students wanted to have sex, they would find a time and place to do that.

Living next door to a person of a different gender didn't automatically mean something R- or X-rated was going to happen. It might. But I can promise you that when I lived in an all-female dorm back in the '80s, plenty of sex was happening all over the building, in cars, or wherever. Not to mention that something made so "forbidden" and "off limits" becomes even more tempting to some students.

Tell your daughter to stay away from boys and watch how quickly she finds them when you're gone. It's just human nature. I'm not saying all college students have sex. They don't even all drink alcohol illegally. However, they're going to do what they want to do. If they don't know how to make good decisions **before** they get to college, they certainly won't want to learn it from their RA or a dorm mom. They may have to learn it the hard way.

Unfortunately, they sometimes make decisions that have permanent implications. All of us in this business hoped we could go an academic year without an alcohol-related death or unplanned pregnancy on our campus. But we didn't always get that lucky.

Not all students show up on campus determined to party their way through their final years as a teen. Many show up determined to learn, meet people, get a degree, watch and play some sports, maybe fall in love, and take steps toward their future.

I've had the privilege of working with some remarkable young leaders, some of whom showed up on campus already that way. I've listened in one-on-one meetings as students realized that what they always thought they should do just wasn't appealing anymore. I've been in those meetings when a student came out to me as gay and seemed to finally relax and get to start being himself. I had a student ask permission to date a fellow board member, and later I got to attend their wedding.

I've had students share with me their incredible faith that they would never force on anyone, but that guided all their decisions and behavior. I had a student whose father was at The Pentagon on 9/11, but that horrible day she was more concerned about our Muslim students getting harassed when wearing traditional Islamic clothing.

I even got the chance one year to hire a 42-year-old undergraduate as an RA, when nobody else thought he'd fit in. He was an amazing RA!

He's the one who, dressed as Barney Rubble from the Flintstones for Halloween, was taking young kids from the community around the dorm for our annual Safe Treat. He came to one of the doors with a "Knock Here—if you dare" sign on it and assumed it would be a good place to stop. After all, nobody got a sign like that from me until they agreed to the rules of how to welcome (not scare) these local kids and agreed to hand out the candy I bought in bulk.

However, these two students opened the door and out poured—literally—smoke from at least two joints.

My RA, Tim, had the presence of mind to redirect his group of kids to further down the hall so they would be spared the smell, and proceeded to skillfully handle the incident with the police—still in costume. That's one we still laugh about!

Chuck and I decided to head back to Texas to be closer to our aging parents, and we chose College Station again. It's one place all four of our children have a connection with, as do we. It's also the home of Texas A&M, where we both received degrees (eight years apart). We moved in June 2012, and it wasn't until November that I finally found another right fit.

Academic coaching

When we moved back to Texas in 2012, I knew I wanted to keep working in higher education, and I knew I didn't want to live on campus anymore. But beyond that, I was open to whatever would be a good fit for me and the hiring department.

I applied to several Student Affairs jobs, including ones in orientation, risk management, and student activities. I did get a couple of in-person interviews, and they went well. However, none of them were the right fit—either from their perspective or mine (or both).

The one I thought I wanted most but didn't get would have given me the chance to work with Rusty Thompson, A&M class of '85, who made a personal phone call to let me know someone else was offered the job. I remember the call vividly, as it was truly gracious and caring. It's even more etched in my mind because a year after we moved to Tennessee, Rusty died from complications connected with a heart attack. He was the ultimate Aggie, having an impact on so many students that most of us can only dream about.

About the time I was starting to wonder if I'd ever get another job, I had a fantastic interview with the founders of a new center that was being created on campus—the Academic Success Center. While my focus had never really been on the academic side of things, the idea of getting to coach students toward success was incredibly appealing.

The hiring supervisor assured me that what I might be lacking in academic experience I could be taught between hiring and the opening of the center a few months later. He said what they needed most was someone who had experience working closely with students, could listen well, and was eager to share the tools of success that students might not already have (or know how to use). I'll never forget the relief and excitement I felt on the back porch of my rental home in College Station when I realized I would get to once again be part of the Aggie family on campus!

I was one of two coaches hired to help select and train the remaining staff, led by some amazing professionals with tons of experience. We found four more coaches, and our team was complete.

I'd never been part of something so new, and it was fascinating to be there and watch how it all came together. I realized quickly that I didn't need to know all the answers. I needed to figure out what the students really needed, and I needed to know where to find the tools so **they** could find the answers.

I quickly learned about study tools, test-taking skills, and classroom techniques that I'd never been exposed to. This was some powerful information, and I was eager to share it with the students!

We set up our offices in the newly renovated YMCA Building, where I had worked 20 years before. We had cubicles—a first for me—and the acoustics weren't ideal for private conversations. But it was a start, and our leaders were always on the lookout for a new and better suited space for us. Which, by the way, they found in about a year.

One thing about opening a new office like that on such a huge campus full of so many traditions—you don't get to just open the doors and watch people line up for help!

We were initially asked to see students who had been identified as struggling academically, whether they were on probation or failing just one class. These students were given a new requirement to get back into good standing with the university. They had to make (and keep) an appointment with an Academic Success Coach.

On one hand, it wasn't great knowing the students were forced to come to us. Some of them, naturally, were resentful about having to be there. Others were grateful to get a chance to make changes. You can guess which ones were easier to work with.

My first year in this role, I had the pleasure of coaching the daughter of someone I went to Camp Arrowhead with! She was as beautiful and as smart as her mom, Lisha, and just needed some better study tools. She did go on to graduate and made good use of what we offered her. How different things would be if they all did!

I do understand how a student can be unwilling to be told how to study. So many of them had recently come from high school, where they didn't need to do much outside of class to get good grades. They showed up at A&M thinking it would be "13th grade," and they were sadly mistaken.

The reality check they had to endure was severe for some! We recommended 2-3 hours of studying outside of class for every hour in the classroom. If a student was taking the recommended 15 credit hours, that would mean they should spend about 45 hours a week preparing for those classes in some way. Can you imagine the looks on the faces of 18-year-olds when they were told that? Even when we told them that studying didn't mean just slogging through the textbook. It could mean just about any useful interaction with the material, the instructor, or other resources. It could be quite active!

It's about time

One of my favorite conversations and activities to do with these students was to teach them about the 168 hours they get each week.

Whenever they heard that number, the students would get a very confused look. I understood that look—it was the same one I'm sure I gave my husband when he threw that number at me!

Why did he do that? Well, back at the University of Wyoming, when I started that full-time live-in position, I was still kicking myself about not having finished my master's degree. I knew I'd need that degree to move on to another position, but I'd been "working on it" since 1986. I was convinced that I just didn't have the time to get that degree. I made the mistake of telling my husband that, and he said, "Oh, so you're using all 168 hours in your week already?"

Chuck is an engineer with an MBA, so I don't usually question his numbers. But I took this as a challenge.

He asked me to find (or create) a blank chart that would show seven days a week, with space for 24 hours each day (basically, a grid). Easy enough.

Then he asked me to color in all the hours that were committed to recurring weekly meetings. He was smart to ask me to color because he knew I was well-equipped for that task!

After I did that, he told me to use a different color and put in an hour for each meal, three times a day. I could see where this was going, so next I chose another color for my "office hours" that were somewhat flexible, but still were a full work week.

He then startled me a little when he said, "Now color in chunks of time for getting ready in the morning, walking to and from certain things you do on campus, and sleep—at least eight hours a night."

I was sure at that point I would fill up all the calendar slots.

I was wrong.

Even after putting in plenty of time for exercise (which I wasn't doing enough of), watching movies, playing board games, and just unscheduled time to relax, I still had empty spaces. Clearly, I had room on that calendar to do a master's degree—which he made me also put on the calendar.

There was colorful evidence that I could finally achieve something I'd been bothered by not having for way too long. And on top of that, the university would pay a good chunk of my tuition and allow me some time during work hours to do some academics if it applied to the job. Because I was looking at a degree in career counseling, there was a lot of overlap. I had plenty of opportunity to talk with students about their major and their hoped-for career paths.

So, that's how I learned about the 168 hours, and the impact of carefully coloring them all in. It's a matter of deciding how to spend your time, instead of just wondering where it all went.

I can't remember a single time when I did this exercise with a student that they didn't have an "a-ha!" moment. Not one.

A vast majority realized they weren't using their time wisely at all and clearly could afford to add some more studying. Others realized how little they were sleeping, and how that was impacting everything. Some even needed to add more free time and relaxation, or they'd burn out.

Most had no concept of allowing time to get from home to the classroom—whether they lived on campus or off. It was almost as if they expected to just magically move from place to place. In the age of Harry Potter, it made sense to ask if they planned to use the Floo Network, a Portkey, or just apparate.

It was a surprise to almost all of them to consider the idea of getting up at the same time every day—even weekends.

"But I get to sleep in on weekends!" they would insist. "That's when I get to make up for lost sleep!"

First, that's not how it works. Contrary to popular opinion, you cannot make up for lost sleep. Once an hour is gone, you never get it back. Sleep debt piles up, whether we acknowledge it or not. That's another thing you should read more about, learning from true experts. It doesn't just apply to students.

Second, I would explain how if they would get in the habit of getting up early on Saturdays and Sundays, they'd have more time to do the things they *say* they wish they had more time for.

If they have an early morning class on Monday, Wednesday, and Friday, but no class until noon on Tuesday and Thursday, I would show-and-tell them the benefits of getting up early on all days. That makes it easier to get up when you *must*, because your body and brain get in the habit.

We also talked about, if they had a math class (and therefore math tests) on three mornings a week, they should use the other two (if available) to practice doing math. The brain will start to adjust to that kind of consistency, and it could become easier to perform something in the morning if they had practiced it in the morning.

I'll admit, many didn't believe it could work. Thankfully, many tried it and learned! That activity had the most impact of any I ever shared with students.

I've come to believe that using time wisely is at the heart of so much personal success.

So many people can be heard saying, "I just don't have time!" I used to say that, too. It's just not true.

We each have the same 168 hours each week as Einstein, Edison, and Leonardo da Vinci had. Doesn't matter your age, size, or income—you still only get 168 hours a week. It comes down to how you choose to use it.

Yes, some people have more commitments, longer commutes, and more demands on their time. But we all have **some** choice about those 168 hours. I just had to teach the students how this could change their lives for the better.

I would offer the idea that they could get better grades with less study time—if they used it wisely. I would also suggest that if they got all the truly important stuff done during the week—as if college were their full-time job—they would have more time for guilt-free fun.

I'd describe a situation where a friend suggests a weekend road trip. You agree to leave Friday at noon, and plan to have everything academic taken care of by that time. Every week if possible. So, even a spontaneous road trip (as college can be full of) would be something you could fit in. All weekend, you could savor the peaceful knowledge that you didn't have to cram everything in on Sunday night when you got back (usually more than a little tired). Others would worry and complain about how much they had to do—but not the student who planned ahead! Sometimes, I was able to convince them how much of a pleasure that feeling would be. And they were ready to learn.

When they were ready to listen, we'd start by walking through a process like what Chuck had walked me through, starting with the have-to items, and working down to the wouldn't-it-be-nice-to-have-time-for-this ideas. We'd fill in everything they could think of, including meals, intramural flag football, and dancing on Thursday nights (it's cheaper, and you can get into places under age 21 that night).

For members of the Corps of Cadets with the most challenging lives—freshmen in the Aggie Band who were also engineering majors—we'd get extremely choosy about what was allowed a time slot!

I worked with a cadet one semester who was fascinated by this idea, and eagerly took it on. I had never been a cadet, but I knew their lives were incredibly full. He offered to color a template for other cadets, showing that it indeed could all be done—even during football season. It was a thing of beauty! This helped me have a similar conversation with students who also had jobs, even if their jobs weren't as demanding as the life of a first-year cadet.

Tools and tips

Often, once a student got a handle on making time-use decisions, things would start falling into place. They were then more open to such ideas as the famous "5-Day Study Plan," Effective Note Taking, and Powerful Test Prep. They became willing to hear new ways to read textbooks that didn't involve bleeding dry their new highlighter. They were even ready to talk about the incredibly helpful "practice test" process.

When they started to realize just how much they could get done if they were planning and using better study skills, their academic world just turned around! I had so many tools they could use, even as specialized as tips for studying history more efficiently.

These are things most students probably don't need in high school, and really have no way of knowing about—unless they'd worked with a college-level tutor for some reason. If your student would like these resources, email me and I'd be happy to provide them. However, so would the college they choose.

At A&M and Vol State, we had materials for people with math anxiety, people who got nervous only on test day, and people who struggled to understand an accent of a brilliant professor. We would even coach them on difficult conversations with faculty or other students, doing a role-play in the office if they wanted to rehearse.

I always recommended building a working relationship with the professors from day one. I'd tell them, "When you panic in December because you're about to get your first D, why should a professor help you out if she's rarely seen you in class?"

I've had many faculty members tell me that if a student sits toward the front, takes notes, and actively participates, they'll gladly meet with the student during office hours (or by appointment) even *before* there's a problem. In fact, those who do develop an academic relationship with faculty often don't run into problems later. They're more willing to ask for help—and get it. Also, once they become known to the professor, they're much less likely to skip class. All of that adds up to better performance.

In fact, my daughter shared with me that she got an "A" on a quiz she missed in Theater class because the professor remembered her speaking up in class, always attending, and going to his office hours in the snow.

I also didn't know anything about something we had at A&M (and other schools) called Supplemental Instruction (or SI, because we made an acronym for everything). An SI leader is a student who has successfully taken a specific class before and is willing to take it again and tutor students in that class. The SI leader must be selected by the faculty member and work with that faculty member all semester. It's a coordinated approach to the classes that most often challenge the most students. The data for how well this works are remarkably positive. I won't include it here, but it's worth a Google. Oh, and at most schools, it costs nothing (beyond the tuition and fees a student already pays).

This is more than just tutoring—it's incredibly specific, and the student is working with someone who truly has won the race already and is willing to share how they did it. The SI program was a partner with our Academic Success Center at A&M, and it was amazing. I'm sure it's in many—if not most—schools in the United States (and probably some abroad). The disappointing thing is that so many students either don't know about it (because they're already bombarded with so much information) or aren't willing to make time for it and give it a try.

We also did workshops at the Academic Success Center on all the most basic and important issues struggling students face. It was so disheartening that the workshops were rarely full. Some professors would give students extra credit for attending, which got some of them there. Others would be strongly encouraged by an Advisor to attend the workshops.

If they stayed awake, stayed off their phones, and participated, they always left having learned valuable skills. And we made it clear that we were there for one-on-one instruction any workday. No extra charge. Just make an appointment and keep it. We'll do all we can to figure out what's in your way and show you how to get above, around, or through it. How I wish more students had taken us up on those offers—before it was too late.

Sadly, there were too many times of the year when we had the free time to clean our offices, check Facebook, and get caught up on our professional development reading. And I'm not talking about the time after the students clear out when finals are over.

Not everyone knows this, but most schools these days operate almost year-round. They have what's called May-Mesters, Winter-Mesters, and Bridge Courses between the "normal" semesters. And as employees—not faculty—we worked every day the campus was open. We did get a great chunk of time for Christmas vacation, though! But one of my least favorite (yet still amusing) questions to be asked was, "If you work on campus, don't you get summers off?" Never. Summer is when we go into wrap-up mode from an academic year, then shift quickly into preparation mode for the next one—with not much of a breather between them.

Ready or not?

Who is it *really* about?

As I've mentioned elsewhere in this book, it's critical to know exactly who the college choice is about. Is this something your son or daughter (grandchild or other) really wants? Is this a family expectation? Is this a legacy issue? Cultural? Societal? Is it "You have to go to college because, otherwise, you can't get a good job?" Is it "All our kids go to State!" Is it something all the other kids are doing? Is it just what happens after high school?

Go back and read those "reasons" again. While more than one may be true, there's only one that can be the driving force for a successful student. **The student must want college at least as much as you want it for them—*if not more.***

The student will be the one going to class (we hope), making daily decisions, and having their name on the diploma. This isn't about you or the family full of alumni or being part of what the crowd is doing. They can't be going to college just to make you proud. Pride in their accomplishment comes after they've done it, with you there to encourage and offer appropriate support.

Let's tackle some of those reasons above. Again—they may very well be true in your world. That does **not** make them the right reason for your son or daughter to attend college right now. First, let's look at family expectations.

Family expectations

Maybe everyone has gone to college, and some even have graduate degrees. Maybe nobody has gone to college, and this is the first chance for someone in the family to do that. Maybe all hopes have been pinned on this child by more than one generation.

Regardless of the situation that describes your family, it's not enough.

Traditionally, those hopes have been a motivating factor for many students. It hasn't always gone well, although I'll admit that it can eventually work. It may not be pretty, and it may lead to some resentment, but I'm not totally writing off this reason.

Just know that in today's world, students know there are a lot more choices available to them. They also know enough to question what their family has always expected. Some cultures are much less likely to question what a family has in mind for them because it's woven into all they do. For those students, it's more likely to work out well. For others—not so much.

One reason it won't necessarily work is that some basic assumptions are being made. The same assumptions that held true 30 years ago (or more) may not hold water now.

When I was in high school, it was just assumed that I'd go to college. It was almost assumed I'd specifically go to Texas A&M. The only question was which dorm I'd be able to find a room in.

Many of my friends had the same assumption—just different colleges. We were all reasonably intelligent and had good grades and plenty of activities on our résumé. Most of us had parents who went to college. Some didn't, but the parents were determined that their children would go farther than they had.

The assumptions I mentioned above include the idea that college can be afforded without massive debt. Sometimes, scholarships are available, and sometimes, financial aid is awarded. But not always.

College is so much more expensive today than it was before. Although I don't know enough about inflation and relative income to know if everything rose at the same rate. I do still have some of the bills from when I was in college, and I guarantee that my daughter's bills were higher (for a state school).

If your child is planning to attend a private school or go out of state, the costs will rise rapidly.

You may have read about the growing student debt in our nation. It's just not advisable to continue to add to that, unless, of course, the return on investment will make it all worthwhile, and relatively soon.

For example, if your son wants to go to a school where tuition is $50,000 a year, he'll walk away with a degree in (maybe) four years, having spent $200,000 to get that piece of paper. That's not including books or other costs of living—just tuition.

If that piece of paper says that your son has an engineering degree, there's a possibility his salary will allow him to pay that off before his own kids want to go to college. If it says something like "sociology" (which is an incredibly important body of knowledge), the rewards our society offers for it aren't as good.

Beyond the financial issues, let's consider the legacy idea. If your whole family went to one school, and your daughter is expected to follow that tradition, what happens when what she wants to study isn't offered at that school? What if she wants to go to the in-state rival school? There are plenty of families in the United States—especially the South—where this kind of decision can split families! I wish I were kidding.

In my own family, my father went to Texas A&M (although he technically graduated from the University of Texas after one semester). My mother *wished* she could have attended A&M, but also enjoyed their first year of marriage in Austin while my dad finished his degree. She even worked on the UT campus and loved it.

My two oldest brothers, born in November 1951 and January 1953, were raised wearing Aggie Yell Leader outfits and Aggie t-shirts. Bud, also known as #1, chose A&M and the Corps of Cadets (only made optional in 1965 and he was entering in 1969). My mom joined the extremely active Houston Aggie Moms club. We went to campus as often as possible, as it was just 100 miles away.

When it was time for Marshall, #2, to choose, my parents wanted him to go to A&M. That's the **last** place he wanted to go, and he was determined to attend UT in Austin. According to Marshall, my parents tried several bribes (including a car) to get him to join #1 in College Station, but he wasn't interested. His attendance at UT made our Thanksgiving Day somewhat tense, as we were a "house divided." (The annual rivalry game was played on Thanksgiving. In fact, #1 was born on a rare day back then when the Aggies beat Texas, by one point).

When it was Eddie's turn to choose, the pressure was reduced a little for #3. He originally chose Sam Houston State (where my son "attended" many years later) but ended up at UT in Austin. Both #2 and #3 are avid Longhorns (and one has a tattoo to prove it). By the time it got to me, several years later, I made it a tie and went to A&M. Over the years, including since A&M left the Big XII and moved to the SEC, the rivalry has continued.

From time to time, it was probably annoying to have kids at rival schools, but it certainly wasn't the end of the world. It surely would have been more convenient to have the first two at the same school when they were that close together, so I can understand that desire. Yet, it ultimately shouldn't matter. *The right school is the one that fits the **student** for the best reasons.*

Cultural and societal expectations

For a long time, the "establishment" didn't expect students in some cultures to go to college. However, the students in those cultures could be as smart and as hard-working as those in others. Often, those students were ignored early on, as not even having the potential for college. That's an even bigger waste than sending kids to college who **are** expected to go, but don't want to.

The historical college attendance of an ethnic group isn't a good reason to decide that students in that group will continue that pattern. Times have changed—though not enough—and students of all groups should have access to an education, if they're qualified and **want** to do the work.

I'm no expert on this topic. But I can tell you I've seen more students from the groups that weren't traditionally expected to go to college work hard and want help. Maybe it's because society looks at them and scoffs at their ambition. Maybe that's enough to spur them on to prove society wrong. I think that it's society's loss if we discourage someone from getting more education because people who look or talk like them didn't usually do it. Some aren't spurred on by the ridicule but, instead, decide not to even try. What a shame. So many bright minds and eager hearts don't even start college much less finish. That must stop.

I'm a strong believer that everyone who wants to and qualifies for college should be encouraged and allowed to attend college if it's necessary for their chosen life path.

That doesn't mean "everyone should get free college!" I mentioned before how I've seen this go wrong.

It seems that too many people see something as less valuable if they get it for free. They have no "skin in the game," so to speak. This isn't just my opinion. I've had many students tell me that they had college paid for and wasted it. When they got a chance to return, using their own money, their level of dedication increased dramatically.

Even adult students in Tennessee who are part of the "Reconnect" program (getting their education tuition free if they haven't yet finished a degree) have told me their entire attitude toward education has changed.

Part of that's just being an adult and understanding what it takes to be a college student. Many of them are grateful for the "free" part and prove that gratitude by extra hard work and excellent grades.

Unfortunately, most 18-year-old students haven't figured that out yet. Telling them that they must go to college because it's "free" isn't making them more motivated to attend. They seem to feel like "nothing invested, nothing lost." And that's what too many students invest—absolutely nothing.

Getting a good job

What about telling students they must go to college to get a good job?

There are many ways this can be true. If your son wants to be an architect or your daughter wants to be a surgeon, they have a *ton* of education ahead of them as well as licensing. That's unavoidable and based on sound reasoning. The training required to do these jobs isn't for just anyone. It requires a certain kind of intelligence (depending on the career) and quite a bit of dedication. It also requires the right aptitude and abilities.

But not everyone wants a career that requires a doctorate or specific licenses only available after a bachelor's degree (or more).

What about those students who love fixing things and are quite good at it? I bet you can name half a dozen or more jobs that you count on in your life that are expertly filled by someone without very much traditional post-high school education.

As I said earlier, I've never asked a plumber where they went to college. I'm much more interested in their training and the reputation of their company. I also want the person who repairs my car to be an expert at car repair—regardless of how much education they have. I'm certainly not interested in seeing a diploma from a prominent four-year university!

I could go on and on. There are many high-paying, necessary, honorable, interesting jobs out there that do **not** require a college degree. As just one example, there are technology related jobs that don't require a bachelor's degree and people with those jobs make good money.

Yes, there are plenty that do require a degree. The point is, students need to be sure they're getting the right one for *them*. And getting the "education" necessary to be good at it and make the kind of life *they* want.

Writing this reminds me of the movie *The Bucket List,* and how intelligent, well-read, and well-spoken Morgan Freeman's character was. He was a hard worker and good at a job that made him valuable to countless people. But we're led to understand early on that his brain is quite powerful, and he's full of knowledge. He also gained a lot of wisdom and used it.

Life didn't give him the opportunity to get degrees to prove it. His kids got that opportunity, though. I'd argue all day that Morgan Freeman's character was smarter than most, if not all, of the college-educated characters he interacted with. He just didn't get the credentials.

How we value people shouldn't be based on the initials after their name, the framed diplomas on their wall, or the class ring on their finger. Their behavior as part of a functioning society should be what matters. Their character. Their treatment of other people, animals, and the environment. We aren't put here to judge. But I think we're indeed put here to appreciate the contribution of everyone who chooses to make one. I'm sure I've seen the best contributions from people who are working in an area that's a fit for their abilities, skills, and interests, maybe even their passions. And they don't always choose at age 18 what will still be a good fit when they're 48.

Follow the crowd

One last item from above. What if college is what everyone else is doing?

Sometimes it's not even "everybody else." Sometimes it's a girlfriend (see earlier chapter about my son). In my case, other than family expectation, I just wanted to be somewhere else with a little freedom. Surely, I'm not the only high school graduate who just wanted out of the house! And what better place than a college campus? Especially when you hear all the stories about how much fun it is!

I'll agree that being with a group of friends can make the transition to a college away from home somewhat easier. It certainly helped me become part of campus life. It didn't help me attend class, though, because none of them were in my major. A lot of people in "friend groups" go to technical schools as well, so this doesn't apply just to colleges. Some high schools even have athlete-style signing days now, or career days for those who want to go directly to a job.

Going where the crowd goes has been infamous for decades as not necessarily a good idea. Remember mom saying, "If everyone else jumped off a bridge, would you do that, too?" The smart-mouth kids among us said, "Probably, because I can swim." That's the point where I usually got grounded. In fact, I think I'm still grounded for something I said back in 1978.

If your daughter has friends who've been active in what matters to them, have strong grades, and stayed out of trouble, maybe it's not a bad idea to go to college like "everyone else" is. But if that's not the case, reconsider.

How do you know the right path?

So, how do you know whether college is the right path for your son or daughter? And keep in mind, it may be the right path—just *not right now*. Regardless, let's look at how to know.

First, let me repeat what I've said several times: *this isn't about you*, parent (or other adult supporter). **This is about the student.**

Yes, you have more life experience, more wisdom, and want what's best for this student. However, **you** aren't supposed to be the one making the choice, doing the work, or asking the questions. If this student spent their childhood being told what to do, think, and feel, then it will be a huge stretch for everyone to shift this to where it belongs. That's a whole set of issues and books and therapists, perhaps, to get to where it's about them.

But with a hopeful spirit, let's assume this child has had some say in what they want, what they wear, how they do things. Let's say their opinion mattered in decisions about sports to pursue (if any), friends, and what academic subjects to focus on when there's a choice. Let's say this child has even had a chance to try something—and fail at it. In ideal circumstances, they've even learned from some mistakes—maybe even with your loving and gentle guidance.

If most of this is true, then the path to some interdependence will be less rocky. Most students fall somewhere on the spectrum between complete autonomy and lawnmower parents.

Some people have more independence than they'd like to have when they're living on their own much younger than they expected, having to earn a living, and even raising younger siblings. Sadly, many also are, in some way, caring for parents in some sort of trouble, illness, or disability.

This book isn't one that can approach those serious topics. The good news is there are plenty of people on college campuses who do have that knowledge and experience. And their entire job is to help those students.

Discipline, responsibility, and academics

The typical student has had **some** parental involvement or control. Sometimes, it feels like interference (but is just responsible parenting). The lucky ones have had parental interest, caring, and discipline, which, as I pointed out, is from a Latin word that means "teaching or learning." I know because I took nine years of Latin (some of it voluntarily).

Discipline might involve some form of punishment, but the main point is to instruct. It can include rules, boundaries, and expectations. It includes consequences from actions—preferably **natural** consequences.

How does this kind of discipline impact academics? Here's a simple example.

When a student isn't overpowered by hovering parents and isn't struggling to live a fully adult life at 17 or younger, they can be taught how to be somewhat self-sufficient. If a high school or middle school student has homework and is told by a teacher how to do it and when it's due, then the **student** is responsible for meeting those expectations.

The student must take the lead in getting the work done and turned in (that's a key point!) on time.

The student can certainly ask for help with a project or problem. But they should **ask** for the help, **after** they've tried on their own.

I don't think parents should have to ask, "Do you have homework today?" or "Have you done your homework?" every day. They should assume the answer is yes, and that it gets done before the student gets to do something fun.

The parents make sure the student has the resources and a spot for that homework, and the spoken and understood expectation is that it will get done before play. Maybe a snack is involved, and the parents are around, if possible, to provide any necessary guidance. They should not do it **for** them.

This "ideal" student also has set up a folder or other container to put finished homework into. They know to make sure it's in the backpack they'll grab in the morning on the way out the door.

With all this in place, if the homework doesn't get turned in, guess who's responsible for that? Guess who gets the grade that reflects that effort? Guess who eventually learns how to follow through on assignments? That's an incredibly valuable skill for an adult to have. This is a great way to learn this, if it hasn't already been learned at home in other ways (chores, animals, small extra jobs, projects, Scouts, 4H, etc.).

When a parent rushes to school with forgotten homework, they've just taught the student whose job it is to remember and that they can be rescued. The same applies to a forgotten lunch (if a system is in place to help produce and remember that lunch). If forgetful hungry students aren't rescued, they'll be a lot more determined to get to school with food next time, I assure you.

These are natural consequences and need to be learned early. Unfortunately, some parents are too afraid of how it will look if their child doesn't have a lunch or who worry what the teacher will think if the student isn't doing homework.

As a quick aside, many students (and their parents) also must deal with the impact of ADD/ADHD. The parents must walk a fine line between helping and helping too much. There are some wonderful resources for these real issues.

One way to deal with worry about how things look to the teacher is to have the conversation at "Meet the Teacher" night (or in an email). Explain the family systems in place, who is responsible for what, and the agreed-upon natural consequences. If you're able to make this work in your world, you're giving your child an advantage over all the students whose parents do everything for them. It's a **huge** advantage.

If you have raised a child with these lessons and boundaries, you're probably not even reading this book. Or, if you **are** reading it, you're doing it so that you can adjust to the differences to be expected at college. You're the parent all the advisors I know are more than happy to see! You're the one who doesn't call on your student's behalf, doesn't ask all the questions the student should ask, and lets your student completely take the lead. You're the parent who realizes who this is about. You're the parent who may not have gone to college but recognizes the value of education. We're thrilled to see you, and even more eager to assist your student.

This family is usually the one in which the student has chosen college for some reason that's important to them. They most likely have been exposed to higher education, maybe even encouraged to think about college. Maybe they went to sports events or a homecoming at a parent's school. Or maybe neither parent got the chance to go to college and both made it clear that it was a priority. Regardless, they grew up with education as a value and obvious support from parents.

Where my first husband and I may have gone wrong with our son was in not only assuming he'd go to college but also in **pushing** it. We assumed he would because he grew up in a college town and was more than smart enough. There wasn't much "choice" involved. We leapt right past the idea of choice of whether to attend and focused on choice of school and major.

I'm sure that at age 17, he didn't feel like it would be easy to bring up ***not*** going, and he may not have even known he wanted to have that discussion. He may have assumed just as we did, that college was next. At no point in his teen years was there a discussion about alternatives, or what it meant to really **want** to go to college. If there was, I don't remember it.

We were perhaps a bit blinded because we both had careers at universities, and we knew our kids were bright. Plus, his sister was about to be a college senior and was doing great. Yes, we knew they were different people entirely. But we just didn't see that an alternative would have been a great idea—or at least a great conversation.

Finding fit

It's hard to say exactly how to know if a student is ready for college, beyond the idea of being able to get into one (or the one they really want the most). There are so many kinds of "ready" in this scenario, just as there are so many options of how to get an education (or go some other direction).

There are some things you can look for that will at least alert you to whether you should be saying "Wait—let's stop and think more about this."

Delay isn't deadly, even though some people are all about "early acceptance" and "getting into the best possible school" and "if you don't go now, you never will." Elsewhere I discuss alternatives to college right after high school, including such concepts as taking a "gap year."

Granted, if your daughter wants to be a surgeon, there are tons of steps along the way that will qualify her to be a doctor who operates on people. No doubt. It goes way beyond just what school and what classes and what grades. But not everyone needs to (or wants to) or can qualify to be a medical doctor. Nor should they. Those are the exceptions—not the rule. Most of us don't have children who will go on to be surgeons.

If you have a daughter who was put on this planet to be a doctor, then she'll have certain kinds of intelligence, aptitude, and interests.

She'll need determination, an incredible work ethic, and a mind that loves math and science. She also won't be squeamish or incredibly impatient. She'll be dedicated to the long haul of college, med school, residency, and figuring out a specialty (or not). She'll need to learn to deal with the nightmare that's our insurance system. She'll need to understand intense personal competition and will learn to exist on very little sleep. (I had a roommate once who was a medical student—I could literally go weeks without seeing her because of her study hours and lab time.) I hate that doctors are expected to do so much on so little sleep, but that's another problem I'm not equipped to solve.

Anyway, it needs to be obvious early on that there's exceptional aptitude of a certain kind and the willingness to do all the work required—and more. And not all doctors go to Harvard. I've also known students who were smart enough and willing to work hard, but the reality of the lab classes was a horrible fit for them. This is where we would have a conversation about why they really want to be a doctor. What's at the heart of that? Wanting to help people? If so, there are so many ways to help people I can't list them all! It doesn't all have to be medical.

Many students have never looked at the heart of their desire to be a doctor. The ***why***. The ones who sometimes struggle the most with changing that decision are the ones who are expected to become doctors because of their culture. Or they're the ones who think it's a great way to get money (and expensive cars). Also, they're the ones who grew up in a medical family and were supposed to step into mom's practice then take over some day. It's tough to walk away from those expectations.

I once had a student come to me at A&M because she was failing her science classes. This was especially problematic because she **had** to get into med school. I asked her why she **had** to do that. She said, "I have to be a pediatric psychiatrist, because that's who made the most difference for my brother and our family when he had cancer. I want to make that kind of difference." Wow—that's compelling.

I asked her what it was that the psychiatrist did that mattered most to her. After she described what made such an impact, I asked her if any of it had to do with prescribing medication or admitting him to the hospital. She told me no. The way he cared and connected with her family is what she'll always remember.

I then pointed out that this person didn't need a medical degree to do that. She asked how that could be. I described to her the position in hospitals of an advocate, or counselor, or patient partner. It goes by many names, and most of those positions aren't held by someone who went to medical school.

We talked about the difference between a psychologist, a psychiatrist, and a counselor, including the education each one required. I emailed a friend who worked at Texas Children's Hospital and she sent me information about the people typically on cancer patient care teams.

There were tears in this student's eyes as she realized she could still help people in that tragic situation. And she wouldn't need to ever go to medical school. It was a life-changing discussion that she didn't even know to ask about.

Why should she have known that? "Career Day" in high school doesn't go into that kind of discussion. We see someone who makes a difference, and we want to be just like that person. We assume we need to do it the way they did. That's so not true in so many cases.

Yes, if you want to cure diseases—actually *doing* the science and/or the physical patient care—you will need a science-based degree of some kind. You don't necessarily need an official "doctor of medicine" degree but something with a lot of science and lab and patient care experience before doing it full time.

I use this example because it's an obvious one. But I want to make the point that we need to try to find out what's at the heart of what a student wants to do or be. Consider these questions.

- What problems do they want to solve?
- What kind of work environment would be a great fit?
- What kind of learning do they respond best to?
- Where do they want to live (if their chosen profession is limited to someplace like New York City, for example).
- What do they want to do on a typical day?

- Do they want to use their hands?
- Do they want to work alone?
- Do they want typical work hours, or do they hate the idea of being a 9-to-5 person?

There are many more questions that are important to consider before picking a path. And, once again, remember **who** needs to walk that path. This book can't cover them all, but there are books devoted to these questions. For example, there are activities that lead students through choosing their strongest values, and there are assessments that can help them figure out their strengths. At Vol State, we would work with students on these before they were enrolled in college, and some high schools cover these topics as well.

From what I've seen, most teenagers aren't even aware that they should do such activities and ask such questions. I'm not sure where and when it should be introduced, but I feel that it should be when they appear open to it.

This may be the best time to point out that whatever path they choose isn't **permanent**!

It's not written in blood or concrete

Decades ago, people were expected to choose a career and stick with it. Work at the same place long enough to get a retirement party and a gold watch. That's just not the norm anymore.

I've come across plenty of students who were hesitant to choose a major because they didn't want to "get it wrong and be stuck." Some didn't even know *how* to change a major or were afraid of the reaction they'd get at home. Some didn't want to hear, "So what kind of job do you think you'll get with that kind of degree?"

Often, I would tell the story from my own family of how many changes we all made from college to career. Now you get to hear it.

My dad, who got his bachelor's degree in petroleum engineering, did that career until his late 30s. Then he went to law school (with four kids and a full-time job) and absolutely loved his legal career until he was forced into retirement in his 80s due to dementia.

My mom got degrees in English and journalism and was a Realtor for over 30 years (while raising four kids).

My oldest brother got his first degree in zoology and went to medical school. Right up until his final year, with an "A" average, when he decided he didn't really want to be a doctor. At that point, he owed the Air Force for paying his way, so he went into the service for a while. After a couple of career moves based on what he did for the Air Force, he then decided he wanted to be a lawyer. So, law school was next, and that's the career he was about to leave for a different one when he got his fatal cancer diagnosis (and we lost him less than a year later).

My next brother chose anthropology just because he found it interesting, and he knew he would go on to get an MBA (he wanted to be in some sort of business). The only negative of that choice, he says now, was having to catch up with some of the math knowledge that was expected of someone getting an MBA.

My youngest brother was working for Marriott when he started college (he worked as a bellman and a driver of visiting pro athletes in Houston). He liked the people in the hotel business, so he thought a career in hospitality would be a good fit. He asked the leadership at Marriott whether he should get a degree in hotel management. After all, we lived in Houston where they have a great program for that at UH. They told him, "No—they'll teach you the Hilton way at that school. We'll teach you the Marriott way. Just get a degree that teaches you more about people." He chose psychology, and it was a great fit. He's been in the hotel business ever since and is fantastic at it.

My first degree was in journalism. Looking back, I wish I'd done a communications degree combined with psychology. When it was time to choose a major, I went through the A&M catalog. I circled any class description that sounded interesting, only after eliminating all the science- and math-based majors.

The major with the most classes circled was journalism, so I picked it. At the time, A&M wasn't well-known for that kind of program, having been founded as an agricultural and engineering school. But I wanted to be at A&M, so there you have it. I did pursue a career using my journalism education, right up until I realized I was doing what I was trained to do (and somewhat good at), not what *lit me up*.

The "Adair Family Education and Career History" may not be common to other families with our background, but I think it's relatively normal. I also know people who've changed their majors (or careers) many times before finding the right one. I've met students who were only in engineering because that's what people in their family were supposed to do—but they hated math. I worked with young people who had absolutely no clue what they wanted to do for a career. It always surprised them when I'd say, "Wonderful! Why *should* you know that?"

Consider this. We are asking young people to make a decision at age 18 that they're not well-equipped to make. I'm sure that when I was 18, I had no idea what I'd be doing when I was 35! Most people don't. The ones who've always known what they want to do (and love the **reality** of doing it) are rare. The ones who struggle to figure it out, change their minds, and find things they hadn't even considered before are probably the majority.

For those who like research and statistics I would suggest reading the December 2017 issue of *Inside Higher Ed* online. Or go to studentresearchfoundation.org and read their article on changing majors from that same month.

I read an article in *Fast Company* online back in May 2015 that in 2025 there will be career choices that don't even exist today. So, how do we expect children whose decision-making area of their brains aren't fully developed yet, to choose a path for their adult lives? That's ridiculous. Even if they did have the ability, they rarely know what the day-to-day world of that profession looks like. Here's just one example.

I got invited to do a presentation to a Public Relations class at A&M about the real world of PR. The students I faced that day were convinced they'd spend a lot of time at cocktail parties, press conferences, and brainstorming sessions with other brilliant minds. The reality is much different, and they were somewhat disturbed and disappointed by what I told them. The glitzy part of PR is the exception—not the rule. But that's what the general public knows about.

The reality of many jobs would be a rude awakening for most young people. But why should they know any different? Have they spent time watching someone do it? Have they had the chance to ask questions (and get *real* answers)? If not, there are few ways to be better informed. They could decide to believe what they see on TV and in movies, but how helpful would that be?

The concept of "internship" is foreign to most students until college. Even those who work when they're in high school (and younger) are often limited to manual labor, food service, or childcare roles. All of these jobs are valuable in our society, but maybe not what students want to do (or are best suited to do). They don't often get a taste of other jobs, which many of them would prefer. Job shadowing is an incredibly useful experience!

My son considered being a paramedic. Then he spent time job shadowing as part of the health science curriculum in high school, and he quickly knew that wasn't for him. Not enough kids get those opportunities.

It reminds me of the apprentice system that used to be much more common (and still exists in a lot of "craftsman" areas). I'm sure there were some apprentices who were just grateful to have a way to earn money for a family. Others were only doing a specific apprenticeship because it was a family tradition. There also were people who used that experience to figure out what wasn't a good fit. At least, I hope so!

When I say "fit," I'm talking about ability, training, education, interest, and maybe even passion. Many people don't get to find something that checks all those boxes. Those who have that chance should take it, but far too many don't for a variety of reasons. *Let's make sure the parents or other support team members aren't that reason.*

There are books, workshops, conversations, and experiences that can walk a student through this process. The best ones make sure a student understands the required education and training before trying to make a living at something. These resources also make it clear what the earning potential is and what it takes to move up. Finally, they expose the student to the realities, the not-so-fun parts of the job, and the environment those jobs are found in. These things matter so much more than most students know.

If I'd had that kind of experience before college, would I have paid attention at that age? I'm not sure. Probably not.

Think back to when you were a junior in high school. What was driving most of **your** decisions about what's next?

- Getting out of the house?
- Making your parents happy?
- Receiving a large paycheck?
- Having cool stuff?
- Being near your friends?
- Changing the world?
- Spending your days doing something you enjoyed (whether at work or not)?

The last one is usually lower on the list of most teenagers. But, finding something you enjoy, that the world needs, that's legal, and that you're good at should be the driving idea. If that's the most powerful idea—for the **student**, not you—then the decisions should make sense.

Preparing for a meaningful (to them), satisfying (to them), useful (to society) future should be the biggest driver of all your student's decisions. **Their** decisions should be supported by your interest and help **when requested.** Connect them with other adults whose opinions matter to them (and whom you respect) and give them some time to ask questions.

More than once, I've told a student something (in my role as an academic coach) and had them understand and embrace the idea. Next, I heard the parent say to me, "That's exactly what I've been saying all along."

Face it. Parents don't have the same credibility in some areas as other adult professionals, just because you're the parent. I was **paid** to give college advice, yet my own son wouldn't hear me! All these years later, he now recommends me to his friends who want an education. But if/when he decides to go back to school, I'll suggest he meet with someone else who has the knowledge I have (and more). It's just different, and I respect that.

Here's another example that might help.

When I was pregnant with my first child, my parents offered to give us a crib they had in the attic. My husband and I had been doing our homework, and working with a parent educator, so we knew about the safety issues with older cribs. When we mentioned them to my well-educated parents, they suggested fixes. Such as wrapping the bars with duct tape to solve the "distance between slats" issue. I was appalled.

They even asked a pediatrician they knew (closer to their age) who then agreed with my husband and me wholeheartedly. She enthusiastically told them to get rid of that crib and listen to me. So, it works both ways.

We have trouble listening to our parents and our children about so many issues, until we learn to respect the areas where they do know more than we do. They're not infallible, but they're going to be better equipped to give advice in some situations.

It's difficult to trust that our young children—even when they're old enough to drive or vote—know what they're doing. After all, we used to change their diapers! We taught them to use a spoon! How in the world can they know how to make decisions?

The simple answer is, they learn to make decisions by making them. And they learn a lot more from making the **wrong** decisions and getting to learn and adjust afterward (without the "I told you so!").

Maybe when you look back, you wish you'd been given the benefit of the brilliance you're currently offering your son. Maybe you were but didn't hear it. Maybe you didn't have a parent with the information you have, so it seemed less important to listen. Maybe you weren't ready to do anything with the helpful information, even if it came from the best expert you could find.

We're so often not in a teachable place when someone has all the answers we need.

But when we recognize that we have questions and that there are several sources of good answers, we can find a lot of help. When your daughter is asking questions, she may be ready to hear answers. When you're asking all the questions, she may be too busy rolling her eyes and sending a text to a friend who does listen. I've seen that a thousand times.

The bottom line is this: your daughter must want it at **least** as much for herself as you want it for her. She must want to learn as much as her instructors want to teach. She must seek the guidance of her advisor. She must be coachable in her sport.

If college is the right place for her right now, there are plenty of ways for **her** to get help from people who have the most and best information, and who are paid to provide it. If it's not, there are plenty of ways for her to build a useful, honest, satisfying life for now (or forever) without setting foot on a college campus or taking a class.

It's not a quick and easy decision, but it's **hers** to make.

That doesn't mean you have to pay for her cozy life at home playing video games all day and eating your food. You decide when she needs to be self-sustaining.

But realize you're supposed to be raising functioning adults—not needy, old, tall children.

Instead, you can have the satisfaction of her being around you because it's a mutual choice to do so, and you both have lives to discuss and share, including a life she chose for herself. It's quite a thrill to be asked for advice and to be **heard** because you learned (at some point) to stop constantly throwing it at her. It took me longer than I'd like to get there, but what a relief and a joy to see it now!

Before we move on to how to get help if she goes to college, please remember (in case I've said it before) that delaying college isn't deleting her future.

Some students are ready, and others aren't. Some are suited, and others aren't. Some want it, and some don't.

Some of my most successful and dedicated students have been those who are attending as true adults, who haven't been to high school in a decade or more. They're ready, able, and appreciative. That's a great combination for college success. Many of them realize they wouldn't have done as well at age 18—and they learn to be okay with that. Many are so grateful they got to raise a family and are now eager to take another path because their kids are grown and on their own. Not everyone beats themselves up (figuratively) about delaying college, but some do.

I tried to pull them through that to the other side, where they can appreciate how much better it can go for them as real adults. Most of them get there. It's so much fun to see a 35-year-old making top-of-the-class grades when he had been convinced that he was "terrible at school." I've also had adults come back to school who were financially quite successful, but they wanted something that required more education for their "next act."

There isn't one right age for college, and it's still not for everyone!

Your background matters

Students can be strongly influenced by the background of their parents, regardless of what that background is.

Some parents who went to college will have children who go to college. Some parents who didn't go to college will have children who do. Regardless, that difference *does* impact what a student knows and thinks about college.

I've known many students whose parents never had the chance to go to college for a variety of reasons. Those students seem determined to get as much education as possible. Part of that grit came from watching mom and/or dad. Yet, I have two kids who had the same two parents, and the same grandparents (and all but one had at least a bachelor's degree). One of them has yet to complete a semester, while the other completed a master's degree.

So, while the parents' educational backgrounds can have an impact, it won't always be the same impact on each child. Let's look at two ends of this educational influence spectrum.

There has been a lot of research in the last decade or two into the first-generation student. There's even an abbreviation higher ed pros use when talking about them: 1st Gens. A dear friend wrote his doctoral dissertation on these students and their struggles. I had the privilege of proofreading it for him, and I learned so much!

I have no personal knowledge of that perspective, because both of my parents attended four-year public colleges, as did all three of my brothers. I was surrounded by people with college degrees.

Some of today's students grew up without college being common in their family. Maybe their parents didn't go to college because it was too costly at the time. Maybe their parents didn't consider themselves smart enough. Maybe the cultural expectation was to raise a family—not go to college. Maybe their parents had a skill set and career that didn't require a traditional university degree.

There are countless reasons why someone doesn't go to college immediately after high school. Some don't get to finish high school or even attend.

Remember that completing formal education isn't **always** a sign of intelligence, work ethic, or dedication to learning. Not all college graduates are smart! Not all people who didn't finish eighth grade are uneducated or any other crass word such as stupid, dumb, or ignorant. The word *ignorant* means "uninformed," so we're all ignorant of some things.

Ignorance is a problem when someone refuses to become informed when it's available. That doesn't always mean going to college.

Unfortunately, too many parents who didn't go to college consider that a failing of theirs. They're embarrassed by their lack of education and can be reluctant to even discuss it with their children. They consider themselves "uneducated" and unworthy of being part of anyone else's education. They often feel intimidated by the entire process, and even scared to go on campus. Knowing what I know, I don't blame them.

On the other hand, a friend of mine told me this. Her brother-in-law told her he didn't believe a word she said when talking about research she was doing, because it was all coming from books—not the real world. There was distrust of the educated who supposedly consider themselves elite.

Some other parents who didn't attend college consider it a personal crusade to make sure their children graduate. They see what they missed, or how not having a degree may have limited their access to jobs or promotions—or even societal respect.

Some places do consider "equivalent" life experience to take the place of some formal education, but in most cases, it's not a one-to-one ratio.

Often, I think that's just foolish. But academia and human resources seem to conspire to keep it that way, deliberately or not.

Yes, I value education—in **all** its forms. I also realize that, in many cases, a diploma indicates that a person has a set of knowledge that can't be obtained elsewhere, or it shows persistence. I accept all that. But I believe our society has overvalued formal education in too many instances.

When I was trying to "move up" in residence life, I was told that without a master's degree, I wasn't qualified to go to the next level. I was almost 40 years old with two children and had worked on a college campus all my adult life. But I was told that someone who just graduated from a two-year master's program at age 24 was qualified, even if they had focused only on classroom education up to that point. Yes, they knew some student development theory that I hadn't studied. I did go on to study that, and it was useful. I'm still not convinced it had more value than life experience, especially when it came time to handle a tough situation with a student.

There's no way to predict how a student has been influenced by a parent's education level. It could be motivational, or it could be a hindrance. Much of that depends on how the parent views their own value. There are plenty of experts on this topic. They can offer much better guidance than I can. Many campuses have offices that serve these specific populations. I encourage anyone who can be called "1st Gen" to take advantage of those resources!

On the other hand, plenty of students have parents who both went to college, sometimes even the same college and they met there. Many students have parents who are fanatically involved as alumni—and not just with sports! Those students have grown up wearing that college's colors—or wearing the rival team's colors (on purpose). They have visited the campus many times and may even live nearby. Their parents have assumed college was the next step for each child—and it better be the **right** college!

These attitudes from parents often can be more damaging than having no experience with higher education. Many times, I've been with a student and a dad, and heard the dad say, "When I was in school..." That was usually followed by a declaration of how it should be today for this student 30 years later.

Too often, these parents don't understand how different things are. Some things we did in college are now *illegal*. Some things available to today's student didn't exist when we were in college.

We had typing rooms in the dorm, with carpeted walls, so the clatter of the typewriter didn't disturb other students. We were thrilled to have Liquid Paper to "white out" our mistakes. Xerox machines were fairly new. We registered for classes by standing in a long line. We hoped to get a spot in a certain class we'd heard was an easy "A" or that we needed to graduate that semester. Our "Google" was a card catalog in the library.

I'm not convinced we didn't have it better in some ways. At least, we didn't have to sort through a million sources to answer a question and make sure it was legitimate. The Internet is full of junk. Students struggle to understand how to use it wisely, even though the library staff (and faculty) is happy to offer instruction on how to do that. Some colleges even have writing centers that will walk a student through how to do effective research. How I wish more students would take advantage of that.

I think that when most parents were students, there were fewer distractions. All the ones they did have are still around, though. Boys/girls, booze/drugs, and pizza/ice cream are still around to keep a student from studying.

But now they compete for student attention with the Xbox, social media, and YouTube.

Many students also have jobs, siblings to help raise, learning disabilities, and hunger. These are real issues that often went undiagnosed or ignored back in the day. Do some people use some of it as a crutch? Yes. Do others try to tell themselves it's an excuse and they should be able to do things like everyone else (when they really aren't wired that way)? Sadly, also yes.

I admit it was a true joy to see my daughter put on her Aggie ring and get her graduate degree from A&M so she was *officially* an Aggie. I also think she made the right decision by not getting her undergraduate degree there. I love my alma mater—with a cult-like scary passion sometimes. But it didn't offer what she wanted in a college right out of high school. She carefully chose and used her pro/con list to the fullest.

It was hard for me to handle that it wasn't **my** decision or her dad's, and I can assure you he handled it better than I did. He didn't attend A&M, though. His bachelor's and master's degrees were from less fanatical schools.

It can't be more important that our student put our "legacy" ideas first. It *must* be more important for them to find the right fit—if college is even a fit at all, ever, or right now. Again—*it's not about us.*

It always amuses me to hear parents talk about how different things are now in college. Yet they still think they can offer the best possible advice for their student, based only on their own experience.

That's flawed thinking.

It's true that some parents had good study skills and did well in academics. Others (such as I) were lucky they remembered to get a degree and were able to squeak by with the grades to do so. My study skills as a young "adult" were pathetic. I think I looked at my roommate's study habits as ridiculous and overboard. She, however, had much better grades in a much tougher subject. I was there to get a husband and enjoy my freedom. She was working on genetics and other biological topics.

When I became an Academic Success Coach, I was relieved that they offered me time to learn what I should have known back then. There are so many wonderful, effective techniques for academic success! The things I learned so I could teach them to struggling students actually made studying take *less* time. I was amazed, as were they, when they listened and tried.

Meanwhile, parents were buying them multiple highlighters, the latest laptop for class notes, plenty of caffeine-heavy drinks, and snacks for "pulling all-nighters." All are bad ideas, and all were common when I was in college (although there were fewer tasty caffeinated products).

Side note: you do **not** need to buy your students a laptop to take notes in class. Yes, they need a computer. But not for in-class note taking. Many studies have shown they will learn more by taking notes using their hands and a pen or pencil. Google that! And a good advisor can give them ways to effectively take notes no matter how fast the instructor talks.

If you were the kind of college student who did everything right, I **urge** you to consider a couple of things before telling your child how to "do college."

Consider any differences in your personalities, strengths, and challenges. Consider the kinds of resources available to them. Consider their academic interests and possible career pursuits. Consider the campuses they like, and how things work on that campus (versus yours all those years ago). Consider their learning style—something I don't think we knew much about a decade or two ago.

You may have known that you learned better by doing something, instead of being told how to do it. Today we would say you prefer "kinesthetic" learning. When you think about it, how many people like to sit in one place for an hour (or more) and be talked at?

Today, I know many instructors who do all they can to make class **not** just a lecture. They consider student learning styles as much as possible. Making the lesson fit for all learning styles in the room is not easy.

If your student learns best with pictures and has an instructor who only talks, they may hate going to class.

It doesn't make sense to go to that professor and insist they do everything for visual learners. But your student can learn to study the way they learn best, even if the class lecture isn't in that format. They can even try to come up with pictures that will capture the words the professor is sharing. This is the time to get creative!

If you're at all like me, you regret adopting the parenting philosophy of "Do as I say—not as I do." It's hypocritical and frustrating.

What if you only tell them how well you did and how you were the perfect student? When they're done rolling their eyes and/or tuning you out, you still haven't taught them how to succeed. What worked for you might not work for them—in their context.

Many parents are stunned to learn that textbooks aren't all hard-bound books these days. When the books are in that format, the parents are often shocked to see the price tag. It's highway robbery! Especially when they're required to buy the "new edition" that only has one chapter changed from the previous one.

Another thing that's different from when many parents were in school is turning in assignments and doing tests online—even if the class is taught in person. Many parents see it with today's middle school students, but just in case you haven't, let me explain.

In this scenario, usually there's a window of time a student can do the test or assignment. The test could become available online at noon, for example, and become unavailable at 8 p.m. that same day. It could be available all semester.

Whenever that window closes, the student cannot turn in the assignment. Even if they get all the answers right at 8:01 p.m., that 8 p.m. deadline means they can't submit those answers. This can often frustrate students and parents. And believe me, it frustrates the instructors, too.

Yes, at times, the instructor can reopen a window when requested. The instructor can offer fewer points for that student because it's late. That's not new—it's just being done on a computer now.

Plenty of instructors still do written tests and grade them by hand. Some insist on seeing all the work. That way, the instructors and students both know how the answer was found.

There are also new ways to cheat, and new ways to catch those who cheat. Sometimes, the consequences are grim.

All kinds of cheating are considered some sort of academic dishonesty, and some schools move immediately to dismissal. Some students are lazy, while some are desperate.

The saddest case I've known was a student at A&M who was caught cheating. He decided to shoot himself in his dorm room rather than face the harsh consequences. It was too much for him. I don't know whether he was afraid of his parents, his professors, or his reputation. He was a Resident Advisor. He knew about the resources on campus for someone who thought there was no other way out. Yet he chose to end his life rather than deal with the results of cheating. That's tragic.

Maybe the consequences weren't as dire or immediate in my day. Or maybe I never had the nerve or creativity to try cheating. Maybe I was never that desperate. I do know that in two cases I earned a "D" in a class because I didn't attend and didn't do enough work to be able to do well on the tests. I deserved those grades. Was I embarrassed when my parents found out? Absolutely. Was there punishment involved? Probably. I don't remember now.

I know they were disappointed, and I know there was nobody else to pin it on but myself.

I'm not sure how many people have that mindset these days. In a world where we sue someone at the drop of a hat, we look for someone else to take the blame for almost everything. Do students still realize their own responsibility in this area? I didn't see much of it.

I saw complaints about the teacher, the textbook, and the test. I heard moaning about the unrealistic expectations of professors. Telling students that they must read the textbook **outside** of class time and do homework on their own time. Students are *furious* about this intrusion into their lives. I heard them say it in the hallway as they walked away from class. They also seem unwilling to take notes in class. Instead they sometimes take pictures on their phones of what's on the board or screen. Most of them never go back and do anything *with* those pictures.

The ones who do bother to take notes are either trying to type them verbatim on their laptop (between web surfing or shopping) or their writing is illegible. Or they don't touch the notes again until the night before a test, if they even remembered to write down the test on a calendar of some kind.

There are many ways to take effective notes, based on learning styles and the type of material. The best methods do **not** take more time. They take planning, listening, and questioning. They take review. They must read the text before the instructor covers it in class, so it makes more sense when they hear it. But I didn't know many students who did this when I was in school. Chances are you didn't either.

Even if you had methods that worked for you, remember that they might not work for your own child.

Notes for history class are much different from notes for biology class. Homework for an art major isn't the same as homework for an electrical engineering major. Both are time-consuming. And this is where it's such a problem that students aren't learning to use their time wisely.

Countless books are written about this topic. I spent large amounts of time covering this for students. It's at the heart of their possible success, and most just don't want to hear it. I'm pretty sure I didn't either—until the real world stepped into my life.

To sum it up, just because you went to college doesn't mean it will be the same for your son or daughter. You may feel like your advice is falling on deaf ears, and you may be right. I know the words that came out of my mom's mouth sounded a lot like that famous teacher's voice in the Snoopy TV specials.

I even have an electronic desk button that makes that noise, from the Charles M. Schulz Museum. I would push it to show parents what students were often hearing.

How often did *you* take *your* parents' advice? Now, factor in all the other distractions of today's world, and get a glimpse of the impact your words might be having. It's not that they don't love you or need you. They may not want or need what you're offering in this case. Back off and steer them toward experts—*when they ask*.

When a parent needs help

At times, parents will want help—and it's appropriate to get it. I've repeated the idea that this is about the students, that parents should back off. However, I'm still a big fan of parents being informed, supported, and appreciated.

Some schools do an amazing job at this, and it's not always the biggest schools. Those larger schools do usually have more resources. They have more specific offices to help certain groups, but just having huge numbers doesn't mean it's done right all the time.

For example, one school I worked at had fewer than 10,000 undergraduate students. It had a strong parent program although no official parent office. They had specific sessions for parents during orientation. They did all they could to start separating the parents from the students when it was appropriate. They had an organization known as Cowboy Parents, and here's what their website says about it:

> *Cowboy Parents is a free organization for UW families! Cowboy Parents offers many ways for families of UW students to get involved and stay connected and informed about what is going on at UW. As a Cowboy Parents member, you can register your email address to receive access to informative e-newsletters, email updates, an online parent handbook, and much more! Active Cowboy Parents members serve as volunteers and on the Cowboy Parents Council, which is a great way to partner with UW administrators and departments to promote student success.*

I recommend this organization, and those like it, having been a member of the leadership council while my daughter was a student at UW.

One of the strongest organizations of this kind that I'm aware of is the Federation of Texas A&M University Mothers' Clubs. Here's what their website says:

> *The Federation of Texas A&M University Mothers' Clubs was organized in 1928 and has grown to include 108 individual Member Clubs located across Texas and throughout the nation. The mission of our organization is "by individual and united effort to contribute in every way to the comfort and welfare of the students and to cooperate with Texas A&M University in maintaining a high standard of moral conduct and intellectual attainment." Texas A&M University Mothers' Clubs are proud organizations, proud of Texas A&M University and proud of the daughters and sons they send to Texas A&M. Aggie Moms are also proud of making a contribution: to the education of their students, to the future of Texas A&M University and to the future of the Great State of Texas.*

At one point, when I was working at A&M, it was common knowledge that if something *really* needed to get done, somebody should contact the Aggie Moms. They could make change happen if they thought it would improve the student experience!

My mom was president of the Houston area club. She even ended up in the *Houston Chronicle* in a story about how far women have come at a school that used to be all-male, all-military. My mother-in-law was a member long after her son graduated in 1978, well into the years when her grandchildren were attending.

This is the kind of connection that many schools are learning to make with parents. Although some schools have been doing it for decades, others realized it was a case of "If you can't beat 'em, join 'em" or something like that.

Many administrators figured that the best way to "manage" the growing number of helicopter parents was to organize them. I'm sure someone somewhere is researching the effectiveness of this practice.

Some schools have official offices on campus dedicated to parents. Some are called Parent Centers, and others are called Resource and Support Centers. Those programs are designed with that school's population in mind, so each will be slightly different. The goal, though, is to keep parents connected in a healthy way.

Colleges have learned that parents are a tremendous source of support for many students. In that case it makes sense to embrace—and harness—that support. The schools also realize that parents with the best information will be useful to the school's goals as well.

A quick search on my computer led to this simple and effective resource for parents (see link below). Their introduction says this:

> *The transition to college is challenging for both students and their parents. Going from high school to college is a major milestone, one that marks the student's eventual transition into independence. However, neither student nor parent needs to handle the transition alone.*
> https://tinyurl.com/rmvnpb3

It's no secret that parents talk to each other and, sometimes, even listen to each other (when they're not comparing or competing). Organizations such as UW's Cowboy Parents makes that an official connection. But there are countless other ways that college parents connect.

The most obvious include:
- Facebook,
- neighborhood groups,
- church families,
- former high school connections (sports, band, etc.),
- service organizations, and more.

Parents who had a student be successful in college are a wonderful resource for parents who are new at this.

When I gave the talk to parents at Vol State, I started with my own credentials (see earlier chapter). Right after that, I made sure to tell everyone that there was an even better resource in the room. I asked parents who were going through it for the second time (or more) to raise their hands.

I suggested the other parents look around and take note of these individuals. I also warned those "veterans" of college parenting that I'd be calling on them toward the end of our session. I asked them to start thinking about things they wish they'd been told when they first started on this path.

It was rewarding to see them start jotting down their thoughts. It was even more helpful to hear what they had to offer the rookies in the room. Most of the time, it almost seemed like I'd paid them to sit in that room and give the right messages. Without exception, they all mentioned that each student is different. They also all had stories of making mistakes and learning how to let their students make mistakes.

The bonus in many of these sessions was to hear parents say that they planned to go back to school to get the degree they never had time or money for, inspired by their own student's experience.

There's no reason to do all this alone.

I strongly suggest finding other parents to talk to. Start by asking what they'd do if they could do it over. I'd also take everything with a grain of salt, because each family is different. Each parent has a filter through which all decisions flow, and that filter may not fit you.

But their experiences—and what they learned from them—can help you avoid those mistakes. Now that we're adults, we're better at not needing to make all of our own mistakes, ignoring those who went before. I encourage you to join or create groups of parents with common issues or interests or with students in similar majors.

Help each other back off but stay supportive. Help each other find answers, develop campus connections, and survive the inevitable frustrations. Teach each other how to let your students fail *safely* and recover. Vent to each other, instead of to the vice president. Celebrate your students' successes and put their struggles into perspective.

It won't come as a surprise that many websites, blogs, and YouTube videos are out there designed for parents of college students. Some of the hosts of these have expert backgrounds, including counseling, education, and health. Others are just very opinionated or are good writers.

Read through a few and figure out which ones meet your needs. Some will resonate with you more than others, whether it's a matter of religion, region, or humor. You won't agree with all of them, but you can learn from most of them.

Again, realize that each student is an individual, and each parent is facing a different set of circumstances. Also, make sure to verify information as "official" by checking with the school. Rumors spread, legends grow, and misinformation multiplies. It's always dangerous to act upon information gathered from an unofficial source, even if it seems like a great "hack" or "work around."

Also, realize that things change. Rules are revised, requirements are refined, and opportunities expire. It's always best to ask questions after you've done a little research on your own. I can't tell you how much I appreciated the prior efforts at research when I was working with a parent or student. It showed initiative, thought, and a desire to get things right.

One resource I found recently has a great foundation and constantly expanding resources. It's GrownAndFlown.com. They've released a book recently as well, *Grown & Flown* by Heffernan and Harrington. I love the title they chose!

Finally, for those of us who still cherish actual bound paper we can hold in our hands and scribble in margins, there are plenty of good books out there. On the resources page at the end of this book is a list of a few I've liked. They're filled with good suggestions and reliable information; although, I'm sure opinions differ and advice is slightly different based on the authors' perspectives, just as my book is based on my odd life as a dorm mom and real mom.

It seems more books are published each year, but that doesn't mean they're better *just* because they're new. Some of the best ones update a previous version, keeping what worked and deleting what didn't. Keep in mind that our world is changing, so a book on this topic from 2012 may seem older than you'd think. Technology is one driver of this issue. But our society is facing some issues not seen before (or at least not at these levels).

Bigger and prior issues

At times, the struggles faced by parents of a college-age student go beyond the normal nerves or fear of no longer being useful. Sometimes, a parent has been dealing with a student's challenging issues for years, including autism, ADHD, and dyslexia (just to name a few). Sometimes with help—sometimes without. Not everyone has the means to get a diagnosis for every real concern. And there is still too much stigma surrounding mental illness and any learning differences that show up in a classroom.

The best cases have a confirmed diagnosis with appropriate treatment made available as soon as problems or as soon as disruptive differences were recognized.

In those best-case scenarios, parents have been working with both mental health professionals and teachers or administrators at the local school for years. There could be specific plans in place and things being done in and out of the classroom to accommodate the student's challenge(s).

Maybe they're working great in elementary school, get some tweaking in middle school, then get more interesting in high school. As the scientific community learns more about how the brain works, there can be more ways to get a challenged student on a "level playing field."

Sometimes it's medication. Sometimes it's counseling. Often, it's both. No matter what the combination of solutions, the issue usually doesn't go away when a child becomes a technical adult at 18.

Sometimes, the issues get dramatically more pronounced as the academic work gets tougher. And the social aspects of being a student become more complicated. I don't have a specific education in this area. But I've seen many students (with and without a supporting family member) who struggle in college more than a student who is considered "on level." I'm sure there's a better term for a student who doesn't seem to have any learning differences, emotional issues, or mental health problems. I must wonder, though, whether the ones *with* something presenting a challenge are the majority now.

I'm not sure whether that's about better diagnostic capability or a rush to make everything a syndrome. Or some of both. I do know that when my brother was kindergarten age, his alcoholic teacher told him he wasn't smart enough, and he had to repeat the grade. He's as smart as I am, and I skipped a grade at that same school. He and I may be smart about different things, but his intelligence should never have been questioned. That pronouncement by a teacher who was soon removed from her role stayed with my brother for over 50 years.

I don't think the teacher's dependence on alcohol was the only issue, though. My brother and I are now both convinced that he'd be diagnosed as having ADHD if he were in school today. Maybe if he'd had a diagnosis and tools to handle his different way of behaving, he would have been able to show his intelligence better.

So, while I'm not a fan of calling all "different" behavior a disorder, I do know there are plenty of diagnosable conditions. If they're managed well, that would contribute to student success (and less teacher frustration).

If there are prior issues, or bigger issues than the "usual" anxiety over college, I can't recommend strongly enough that the student get help. If it requires parental intervention because the challenge is that severe, then I'm all for it.

What I'm *not* at all for is the rush to **rescue** a student before they've tried anything or taking a direct leap to blaming the teacher or the school when they don't get good grades. And as I've said before, turning 18 doesn't make things magically disappear. Maybe coping skills improve as a student gets older and learns more about how to handle things, but there's no pill to change the wiring in our brains—yet.

There also can be issues that aren't about bodily processes but are instead about trauma in a person's life. People react to things differently, and at different times.

Here are just a few of the issues that can impact a student's ability to be successful in school:
- divorce
- death
- food insecurity (wondering where their next meal will come from)
- family illnesses
- emotional abuse at home
- depression
- social isolation
- battle trauma
- constant family relocation or housing and transportation insecurity

Telling someone to "get over it" or "pull yourself together" isn't helpful.

I'm not a fan of wallowing or whining, but I'm a *huge* fan of getting mental health assistance. I've been using mental health professionals since college in one way or another, and they made all the difference. I still must do the work, but their guidance is beyond valuable.

In fact, I don't know anyone who wouldn't benefit from quality counseling. Notice I said **quality**. Choosing a licensed counselor with the right specialty who feels like a good fit can truly have an impact on how successful the therapy is. Someday, maybe our society will accept using these services as easily and as quickly as we accept visiting a medical doctor to get a prescription. Probably not in what's left of my lifetime, but maybe.

Faculty, staff, and administrators at colleges aren't given a list of people who are dealing with any of the challenges I've mentioned above. They only know if they're told by the student (or the parent in some cases). Once a student self-identifies and provides documentation, a college can provide a tremendous amount of help!

It saddened me to see students unwilling to ask for help, because they thought adults just "handle" things like this. Or they don't want to be labeled as "odd." They don't want pity, but they need some assistance! Keep in mind that the challenging issues a student faces in college impact them much differently from when they're "children" at home, going to grade school.

Many of the students I've worked with have credited their faith-based community with making a huge difference in their success. Parents also can use these resources if they have such a community to rely on.

Not only might a pastor or other church leader be helpful, but other parents in the faith community may have "been there—done that" and have helpful tips. Larger congregations may even have groups for this stage in life. If they don't, they should!

Plenty of resources are available when you have toddlers, such as MOPS (Mothers of Preschoolers). You can find groups for "empty nest" parents—those rejoicing and those in mourning—as well as for those who have children between school age and adulthood when the nest isn't exactly empty, nor are they still in the thick of it every day. If there isn't such a group in your faith community, consider forming one! I know the support would be helpful!

How do you get help?

First, who is the help really for?

Before I tell you more about where to get help on a college campus, first let me reiterate a couple of the most important points of this book.

Make sure the person who needs the help is the person asking for it.

In other words, the student should make the phone call, ask the questions at the office, or send the email. The student is the focus—**not** the parent. Unless your question is related to a parent issue, such as where to meet up with other parents, you shouldn't be the one asking.

Too many parents have spent years doing all the talking for their children. All. The. Talking.

In my view, this can teach the children that they're not capable or that they need not bother to even try. Or maybe it lets them off the hook for thinking or learning to express a concern. Either way, it's not teaching students a critical skill. They must learn to ask for what they need politely, succinctly, and respectfully. Then they must learn to stop talking and listen to the answer.

I've heard about some kids today not being able to communicate in person without technology, and it's a growing concern in the workplace.

Some say kids aren't being taught or made to interact one-on-one, face-to-face. That's another crucial skill they're missing.

I should back up here. Before finding a person to get an answer, a student's first task should be to consult the official word of the campus they're interested in. That official word these days is found on the college's website. Full-time employees are paid to keep it up to date, even if sometimes they get behind.

Years ago, universities printed official catalogs. The one I was coeditor for at Texas A&M was an inch thick, with small print and very few pictures. The amount of proofreading, approval, and fact-checking we did to make sure it was accurate was staggering.

We had color-coded editing systems. We had sign-off procedures that went all the way (sometimes) to the Texas Higher Education Coordinating Board in Austin. Other times, they needed Department Head and Dean approval. I can guarantee you the administrative staff was involved in the nitty gritty of that process.

Today, that's all available to you 24 hours a day online (unless the website is down for maintenance or power outage, which happens). Almost all the most common questions can be answered by doing a search on the college website.

Yes, sometimes the information can be outdated, or appear contradictory. In that case, you want a human to clarify. When you do a search on a college website and it brings up a result from the official catalog, make sure you're seeing the **current** catalog. Sometimes, it's called a bulletin or something else.

Why does that matter?

The catalog is considered the official word of a campus. Students are "subject to" or "under" a specific catalog based on when they enroll. Some schools say your catalog changes when your major changes. Others don't. It matters because, each year, it's possible that important things have changed, usually after going through a rigorous and detailed review process.

Those changes can mean students are no longer required to take a class they were dreading. Or it could mean they need to take a new class that didn't exist before. Those are two examples of what it can mean, and it matters! Too many students don't know about the whole idea of a catalog, much less the consequences.

Which leads me to one of my all-time least favorite phrases uttered by a college student: "Nobody told me!"

I'm not sure if this comes from a lack of responsibility, a culture of blame, or laziness. It makes me nuts!

Colleges tell students so many things in so many ways, and, most of the time, the students aren't listening. They get messages in print, on the Web, and in person at meetings. They even get a text these days from most schools. But because they're getting so many messages all the time, they tend to filter out some of the important ones because they're just not important to the student right then.

There's a concept called "just-in-time information," and it's a tough thing to do. How do you make sure you're telling students only what they need right then (or soon)? How do you make sure not to overwhelm them at the start and trust that they'll listen later when there's more to know? If you figure that out, you can make a fortune. And make sure to share it!

It would help so much for students to speak up and ask for help, after at least trying something on their own. They can Google, right? And let me repeat my major point—the student needs to do this work, **not** the parent!

So, as a parent, if you have a question about something that has to do with your child and their college education, ask yourself **who** needs the information. Ask yourself what the consequences will be if they don't get the information. Ask yourself what they might learn from the consequences. If they always have you taking care of everything, why would they need to learn how to do anything for themselves?

Here's where I have to say something that might offend some people. But I feel so strongly about it that I must.

Being needed is great—but *being wanted is better*. Knowing you've taught your child to be capable, resourceful, and accountable is so satisfying!

There are some parents, though, who seem to be afraid to let their kids learn to do things for themselves because then, the parents won't be "needed." They lose a primary and important role in their child's life.

What they might want to consider is developing a new, different role.

I can't describe how gratifying it is when my kids tell me about something they've done on their own. Or they're considering doing something and want to discuss it with me to get my perspective. They ask for my advice, based on my experience, which comes from plenty of mistakes as well as many years making those mistakes. They also trust that I have their best interests at heart (not my *own* interest of being needed).

We're supposed to give them roots and wings. We're supposed to raise eventual adults who are responsible and interdependent. That's different from independent, by the way. Interdependence, defined loosely, is voluntarily relying on one another and working together.

If we don't raise this kind of adult, we're not doing them, us, or society any favors. That's my opinion, and I'd love to find some science to back it up. Maybe that will be my next research project!

Meanwhile, please consider a different kind of satisfaction. Watching your former children become contributing members of a better society. Knowing you helped shape those adults. It won't be easy to watch them stumble, fall, and fail, ever. But it's worth it.

Start out with "safe" ways for them to fail and go from there. Start with such things as household chores, play, and personal care. As they get older, they can learn from more complicated situations.

Know that when your child is at college—if that's the best path for them—there are so many people there to help them. And those people can't discuss your student with you anyway (remember that information I gave earlier on FERPA). Be there if they **need** you and be careful how you define *need*.

Let me share with you a message I received from a recent graduate that speaks to this idea from the student's perspective. Just know that when I got it, I sent her a message, telling her that her parents are heroes in my book. I hope Suzy continues to let them know how grateful she is for how they raised her.

> *"After my quick semester as a Teaching Assistant, I can't believe some parents actually emailed me! The TA! For their ADULT student! I don't know if it's helpful but from a student's perspective. My parents yelled as they drove away on move in day, "Call us if you're in the hospital, jail, drop out, or change your major! We love you!" and there I was, 1,000 miles away alone as a 17-year-old in college. No, I'm joking, but I'm really grateful my parents slowly stopped parenting in middle school/high*

school. My mom always said our family was a team not a kingdom. We all worked together as a team, and my parents weren't the rulers. (There were a few times I came to dinner with a PowerPoint presentation to explain and convince them on whatever crazy idea I had! Can you believe they let me work in Jamaica as a summer camp counselor when I was a junior in High School!?) I think my parents just trusted that the world would teach me bigger lessons than they could explain them. Stuck in NYC? Well, that's a good time to learn how the subway works. Car broke down in high school? Now is a good time to learn how to call AAA and learn how to change the oil! Debit card expired and I was super embarrassed when my card was denied buying a sweater? Well, that's a lesson on how credit cards expire! Anytime a teacher marked my test wrong when the answer was right, my parents prepped me on how to talk to an adult and an authority figure with confidence. And how to nicely, politely explain my side of the story. Did you break your finger? Well, here's what hospital bills look like. (Thankfully, they covered me for that time! Now I know that stitches are SUPER expensive!). College wasn't a hard adjustment for me because I spent my childhood going to summer camp or grandma's house for months at a time. I don't know, but even kids I went to undergrad with in 2010 were CLUELESS about basic life!"

Where to get help

Higher Ed professionals

I sent out a Facebook request to friends I know from working in higher ed. I was seeking stories, guidance, and support for this book. None of them even knew I was writing a book, although they've known for months that I was no longer working full time anywhere in higher ed. Some may have even wondered what I've been doing all this time, other than travel. Here's the message I sent out:

> *After taking my first summer off since 1982, I've spent the last few weeks doing something I've wanted to do for years. I'm about 25,000 words into writing my first book! The book is designed to help parents*

successfully navigate the deep (and sometimes scary) waters of having a college-age child, whether that child goes to college or not. Based on years in higher ed (including 11 years living in a residence hall as a full-time professional) and having two of my own go through that phase, I'm compiling "insider" information for those who either aren't there yet or who are already struggling with it. Of course, I don't have all the answers or all the stories! I know so many of you who could add to this book, and I'm inviting you to email me and get started. Your true stories, lessons learned, and helpful suggestions can make a positive impact on readers, and you can have credit by name (if you choose). Just give me the facts, and I'll do the rest! Email me, and let's work together to help parents (and other supporters). If we can do that, we can help the students as well! Thanks in advance for anything you choose to offer. I look forward to all I'll learn as this exciting process continues!

I quickly learned two things. First—Facebook only lets you tag 50 people at a time, and second, I found 159 people (and I'm sure I missed some) who fit the higher ed connection!

Some of them are former students of mine. Some are former colleagues. At least one is a Division 1 university president, and at least one is a Division 1 athletic coach.

The list includes professors at universities and community colleges, motivational speakers who spend a lot of time with college students, and people who devote their work lives—and beyond—to helping college-age students and their parents. It included my first cousin's daughter, who's teaching while pursuing her doctorate, and her dad, who's an engineering professor. Several former bosses are on the list as are people I had the privilege of advising and/or traveling with for student leadership purposes.

While I hoped to hear from many of them with their stories and more, my favorite response so far was just this: "Yaaaaaaay!!!!" And this person is aware of how I feel about extra exclamation marks, and extra letters! But her support was a spark for me to keep going, and a reminder of how many people out there "get" what I'm trying to do.

I share this experience so that you'll know the commitment level I've been surrounded with my entire career. It may have intensified when I was part of a live-in professional team. But almost everyone who chooses to work on a college campus has a level of interest and dedication that impresses me even after all these years. Nobody does it to get rich or famous, I assure you. We used to joke in Res Life that we chose the live-in job for the privacy and profit. Ha!

Sometimes, we get lucky and hear from someone we were able to help. Most of the time, we don't.

We give our best whenever it's asked for, and we hope it's the advice or help they needed. We continue to be trained and learn from our mistakes. We go to conferences in our "down time" and soak up the experiences and suggestions of fellow professionals. We share stories that nonpractitioners wouldn't believe.

The only reason my husband believes a lot of it is because he lived in the dorm with me for those 11 years (while running a business of his own). I wish we had a dollar for every time there was a knock on our apartment door (which sometimes was his office), and a student or parent wanted an answer from him.

He came up with a standard response for them, politely letting them know he wasn't the professional on staff. He was just another resident who happened to be married to the area coordinator. Unless, of course, he was 100% sure of the answer. For example, he was good at directing people to the dining hall, or to my office 50 feet away.

Many times, in staff meetings or one-on-one meetings, I had a conversation about how frustrating it could be to try so hard and see no results. At those times, I would be reminded why we do it, and how we were making a long-term investment in people who might not be ready to accept it.

We would often talk about those times we did get feedback from a student—good or bad—and what we learned from it. Working for college students is usually not a quick-reward occupation! Occasionally, it is, and that's a true delight. But most often, you wait years before you learn that you made an impact—if ever.

When we're *truly* tired (e.g., August and April), it can seem like we've answered the same questions a million times in a week. At that point, we must be reminded that it's usually the first time **that** person has asked the question, ever. We try to make good FAQ lists (FAQ = frequently asked questions, for those who haven't spent a career making an acronym out of everything). We try to be patient as we explain that some things we can't answer. We take deep breaths when we're being yelled at for something beyond our control. And we save the eye-rolling for private quarters when another parent has told us their child would **never** do what they were found doing.

Each time we get ready for a new academic year (meaning *all summer*), we get our hopes up again that, this time, we'll do things right. This time, we've learned from all our mistakes. This time, the parents will appreciate us, the students will ask for help, and the incident reports will be few. Then, reality hits.

The reality hammers home that they're still 18 and we've gotten a year older. But we know we chose this profession because we believe we can positively impact the lives of students and their families. We feel certain that if they'd give us a chance, we could help. We're convinced that our degrees, our training, and our heart for helping will impact someone. We know the hours are long and the gratification is usually delayed. But we do it anyway.

As I mentioned in another chapter, professionals on college campuses are making a difference in so many ways. I could list all the jobs—some of which seem menial to some people—but it would take up so much space. To give a couple of quick and obvious examples, I'll mention two that most people know about.

First, I'll talk about faculty. Everyone realizes there are teachers in the classrooms (and online). Although they're not usually called "teachers" at this level.

Some have a doctorate and have earned the right to be called Doctor.

Others are still working on those excruciating degrees but have earned a master's in something relevant. Some may never get to that level for whatever reason. But they're spending time, effort, and intelligence trying to connect with students.

They may seem to have great hours and flexible schedules. The 8-to-5 crowd often harasses them about it. But they don't leave it all at the door when they head home, not even close.

They get up in front of that class (whether in person or not) and offer their experience, their knowledge, and their heart. These days, they do all this in competition with smart phones, short attention spans, and heightened sensitivity (some of which is quite real). They don't get paid a fortune, unless they're long-tenured full professors at major universities whose research finally paid off. When they feel like they've connected and ignited some learning or inspired some change, they rejoice!

They share it on Facebook (names excluded), tell each other about it over coffee, and go home to let a significant other know they had a day that made so many others worthwhile.

Next, let me tell you about the front office staff.

The front office staff in most departments on a college campus are the true "front lines" of college employees. I was once told that working in residence life was like being in the trenches. But I always had my apartment or my office (sometimes, with a front desk staff of its own) between me and the "customers."

From 8 a.m. to 5 p.m., the people you see when you first walk in the door are the ones who can make or break a student's impression of that office.

The students who were "raised right" know that these individuals are powerful. They can be gatekeepers or facilitators. They often know a lot of the answers that the people behind an office door know—and they're easier to get in touch with. They know who's who and what's what all over campus, and they communicate with each other (in organizations and informally).

If you're sincerely nice to a front desk employee, listen carefully, and even write down what they tell you, chances are you'll do well. Try not to ask questions whose answers you could find by Googling. Avoid saying, "Yeah, but my friend told me..." or "Yeah, but I heard that..."

Stand in line, if there is one, patiently. Realize that, most likely, you're not the first person they've served that day, and usually aren't the last. Understand that they've heard the same questions a million times and are doing their best to remember that you aren't the one who asked it all those times. Be aware of when they're on the phone and attempting to work with someone who called instead of coming in. And, whatever you do, don't interrupt when they're trying to help you.

These individuals can be called "receptionists" or "secretaries" in some places, but over the years, those terms have gone out of use. I'm not sure it was necessarily demeaning to everyone. But it's more respectful to use terms such as "administrative assistant," "office manager," or whatever their nameplate might say.

Regardless of their title, they're employees who can be your key to getting what you need. Don't "use" them for this but realize how useful it can be to be on their good side!

Most departments on a campus have front desk staff of some kind, and some have several layers. If you're hoping to meet with a dean or department head, chances are one of those extra layers will present itself.

Keep in mind that, often, these individuals are asked to field phone calls, handle walk-in questions, update the schedule of their supervisor (and maybe others), work on projects given to them with strict deadlines, answer a gazillion emails, and find a chance in there for a restroom break and a cup of coffee. They do have occasional "down times," but they're rarer than you'd think.

Thankfully, my parents taught me that a front office staff member is as important as the president. They just don't get the compensation or recognition in most cases.

If it's a good situation, their boss realizes how critical each of them is to the smooth running of their program. Too many students, though, act as if this is a minion blocking their way to someone who matters. That couldn't be farther from the truth.

Another thing I remember my parents teaching me was to try to get a problem solved at the "lowest" possible level. I'm not wild about the word *lowest* in this case, but when they taught me, it was the 1970s. I don't like the implication that someone is "above" or "below" someone else, even if an organizational chart makes it look that way.

Anyway, start with the person out front in the appropriate office, and don't demand to see the "top dog" right away. So many times, I had a parent or student demand to talk to a vice president as soon as something happened. I wonder if they realized that the vice president was going to refer most issues back to the person in a position to best handle it. That person usually is a front-line employee.

Some places use the term *staff* to differentiate these kinds of employees from "administrators." Those administrators often have much more important titles, larger offices, and a bunch of people reporting to them. They often have the words *Vice* or *Director of* in front of their title, and they spend a ton of time in meetings! They're virtual fire fighters. They're called upon when things get out of hand or when a decision needs to be made by someone with a higher altitude view of the issues.

The ones I've worked with would much rather be in fire *prevention* mode, making sure their "direct reports" and on down the line are equipped to solve problems as efficiently as possible without "kicking them up the chain."

Bottom line: it's about respecting people in any job. *Nobody is beneath you.* Everyone deserves kindness, consideration, and the benefit of the doubt. We never know what someone has already handled before we enter the scene—whether it's personal or professional (or both). We have no clue about the battles they're asked to fight every day on behalf of students, faculty, and administrators.

In my experience, the best front office staff are around a lot longer than some of the administrators and know so much it's frightening. Having them on your side is a great advantage!

Campus offices

Every campus I've been to, worked at, or lived on had a variety of offices set up to help make a student's path easier.

Some of those offices are bombarded by students on a regular basis. Others have seasonal "mad house" times, and others hope the students will eventually learn to take advantage of their services.

Some of those in the last group find ways to compel the students to come in and they hope word will spread that such services are available, useful, and easy to access. Sometimes, that "compelling" is finding a way to require students to visit the office if they meet certain criteria.

Another way often used is a "scavenger hunt" in college success classes. Students get clues and must go to the office that can answer the question. They're required to get a signature or a business card from that office in some cases. We had to get quite creative to connect students with services they could use.

More than once, I remember, in a "slow" time of year, wishing the students knew how much an academic coach could help. But I also learned that a student who was forced in some way to work with me was more than a little reluctant to be there.

Occasionally, I was able to shift that attitude when I did offer them something that they didn't even know was available. It's not easy, though, to shift a student from resistance to eagerness! It's hard enough to shift my own attitude.

What I often found is that if students had been given tips on how to be successful, they got those tips when they were being given too much information at once. They were often offered the information when they weren't paying attention, or they were shown how to use tips they didn't yet need. It's difficult to always deliver this kind of information "just in time," yet that's when it's most likely to be effective.

Too often, an academic coach meets with a student when that student is looking at a 1.0 GPA instead of the 4.0 they had in high school. They're either ready to quit or sick of the whole idea of school.

So many of those students never bothered to return after the first semester of failure either because they'd never been taught how to learn from failure, or they didn't realize they could make it up and still be successful.

The other day, I got to tell a student she could retake a class she was failing and only the newer grade would "count." The "F" would stay on her transcript. But she would now have a built-in answer for that question we all get asked in job interviews: "Tell me about a time when you failed at something and learned from it."

She was stunned to learn that there was a "do-over" available to her. The only reason she even got this information was because she was dating my son! So even though I'm no longer employed by any school, I can't help but go into advisor mode when I'm asked a question. The coaches I've worked with would all happily reveal this "secret" and many more to a student willing to ask. Chances are they have a helpful handout or a workshop already prepared.

The most rewarding part about this incident was that my son told her she needed to talk with me and that I'd know how to help. This is the same son who used to ignore what I had to offer.

Larger campuses have so many offices designed to help students that it's staggering. It can be overwhelming trying to figure out where to go or where to go first. And so many students aren't taught how and when to ask for help! They must learn that calling mom or dad isn't as helpful as calling an office dedicated to their current academic (or personal) struggle.

A quick side note here. I mentioned universities above, and it occurred to me that not everyone knows the difference between a college and a university. Why should you? It's part of the massive and strange vocabulary we tend to use in higher ed.

A university is an institution made up of colleges. For example, Texas A&M University has a College of Agriculture, a College of Engineering, and so on. Sometimes, those colleges are named for individuals who donated a lot of money or achieved amazing things in their profession. For example, Texas A&M has the Mays Business School, named for Lowry Mays, founder of Clear Channel Communications.

A college that isn't within a larger university is made up of divisions or departments, depending on how that school system chooses to name things. For example, I worked in the Business & Technology Division at Volunteer State Community College.

There was a time when schools of this type were known as "Junior Colleges," but that term has mostly disappeared. One reason for that is these schools focus not only on traditional undergraduate education but also on educating members of the local community in some way. Their admission process is more open and "rolling" (meaning you can usually register for classes right up until the first day of class) and less costly. Other differences exist between colleges and universities, but these are the most important ones for this book's purposes.

It might be helpful to know the difference between public and private, and between four-year and two-year schools. They're somewhat self-explanatory, but not always.

Some would say that public colleges and universities are funded by the state they're in, but that's not entirely straightforward. At one point, when I

133

worked in PR at a university, we made it clear that we were state *assisted*, not state funded. One is partial, and the other is complete. We had to find other sources of income to keep going!

Most private schools are:
- more expensive,
- more exclusive in their admissions,
- have different rules and requirements of employees and students,
- and have different funding sources.

Often, they're connected with a religious organization of some kind, which has a strong impact on how things work.

Remember, there are many ways to figure out whether a school is a good fit for a student, and prestige is rarely enough!

Almost all schools have offices for admission. Sometimes, they're combined with an office that focuses on student records (but not always). These offices do work together, whether they're housed in the same place or not.

These offices produce and process the applications for admission and keep track of all the relevant records for all students. That includes at least:
- standardized test scores,
- high school graduation verification,
- previous college coursework,
- relevant military information,
- citizenship,
- contact information,
- immunizations, and more.

You can imagine that this office has its busier times, especially if there are deadlines for admission.

There are always deadlines, but some schools have earlier and more definite dates.

At Volunteer State, we would allow a student to apply and enroll in a class if that class had not met twice. So, if they wanted a Monday & Wednesday class at 10 a.m., they could register for it at 9:55 a.m. on Wednesday, assuming all the right paperwork were in the hands of the admissions office.

Admissions offices don't sit and wait for people to walk in and want to apply, though. They do quite a bit of outreach. That can include high school visits, college fairs, community events, mailings, and more. At the bigger schools, they have recruiters who have territories or special populations they target. Most schools want to make sure everyone has a chance to at least apply and know what's available. That's a year-round job.

Another office almost all schools have is an advising center. Even at large schools where there are advisors in each college or department, there is often a central location for any student to get help.

This office is the one everyone seems to call for "advice," even if there's a specific office that usually handles certain questions and it's clearly named such as "Admissions." In the advising office, we forwarded a lot of calls and people to the better office for their issue.

Advisors are there to help students navigate such decisions as:
- what to major in,
- what classes to take in what order (that's usually spelled out in the student's official catalog),
- how to survive a tough class,
- how to work well with faculty members, and
- how to understand where to go for more help.

Too often, students want advisors to make decisions for them or tell them what to do. I had a sticker on my office bulletin board that said, "I advise—*you* decide!"

What can make an advisor thrilled is to have a student come in and tell them that they've already looked through the requirements, done a little research into the classes, and put together a couple of possible schedule combinations. They just want to make sure they're on the right track.

Yes! Good for her! She tried something and most likely learned. If she has questions at that point, we're eager to help find the answers!

The advising office is also sometimes the place to have discussions about what a student wants to do when and if they grow up. They're not the career center. But they can usually provide some assessments to see what's a good fit. That can happen while they're in high school or while they're in college.

They talk with a student about aptitude, what's required in majors, and where to get more information. They shouldn't be expected to tell students what to major in, how much money they'll make, or where to get a job. Many of them *can* share so much about how to study better, take effective notes in class, and manage a challenging schedule. That could also be in a student success center at a larger school, but many of these responsibilities are shared.

Make sure the student is talking to the best resource for the issue.

For example, I wouldn't answer any questions about financial aid unless I had a handout provided to me by the Financial Aid office that would apply to all students the same. That information changes often, is specific to each student, and was way too important for me to make an educated guess.

Speaking of financial issues, there are overworked professionals in that area! They're often combined with the scholarship office but not always. They can't answer a parent's questions about finances, even if that parent is paying for school, without the student's (usually written) permission, unless that student is under age 18. This is a federal law, not a way to frustrate parents. Yelling at these hard-working employees with, "Dammit—I pay for his education, so you'd better tell me what I want to know!" isn't going to get you anywhere. And it's not fair to those employees.

Hostile parents often get to meet the campus police in these situations and get to hear more about FERPA.

Financial aid is often the most frustrating things a student (and parents) can face. First, there's the FAFSA (Free Application for Federal Student Aid). Some states are now requiring FAFSA applications for high school seniors. There are hard deadlines, masses of paperwork, surprise audits, and inflexible requirements. I promise—none of this is created by the financial aid office employees to make your life more complicated!

Please try to understand how many people they're trying to serve, how many regulations they must remember, and how many times they've dealt with the same issues. It's a thankless job sometimes, and I admire those who continue to do it with a smile. Know that if there's a dollar sign involved the student needs to talk with a money-related office.

It could be called the Bursar's office, the Financial Aid office, the Scholarships office, the cashier, or some other money-related name. Usually there's a Frequently Asked Questions (FAQ) section on the school's website that will tell you where to go with what issues.

One office that gets underused, in my opinion, is the group that helps students with some sort of disability. Unlike in grade school, this office doesn't start off with information about the student who needs accommodations. Students must self-identify and ask for help.

Another former student of mine, Heather Welch Tottingham, told me this story to highlight that point.

> *When I had stress fractures in both feet and used a wheelchair for three months, I contacted this office about one of my classes which was scheduled to be taught in the basement of the History building. It just so happens that this building doesn't have an elevator. I contacted them and they were able to move the class to a building and room that I could access while using my wheelchair. It was so empowering! Everyone was wonderful about it, especially the professor. I actually had two classes back-to-back with that professor, the first being the class that was moved. Every Monday, Wednesday, and Friday morning, I wheeled myself to the first class, and then he gave me a push to the second class. With only 10 minutes between the classes, and the distance between the buildings, there was no way I could have made it on my own in time. But the professor was more than happy to accommodate me and make sure that I could attend both his classes. I think back on this experience often and remember not only what a humbling experience it was to have a temporary disability, but also what a wonderful experience it was to have so many people willing to make minor adjustments in their lives and schedules in order to accommodate me and set me up for success.*

Sometimes, a student will think or say, "Well, now that I'm in college, I figure I'm an adult, so I should just deal with my dyslexia." The sad truth is, dyslexia (and other challenges) only get harder to handle with the college workload. It doesn't just go away!

Often, students and their parents are worried that the student will be labeled in a negative way. If a student truly needs extended time or a quiet surrounding for test taking, that student must have documentation that says so. That documentation must be given to the professor, or the professor won't know it's necessary. Parents were usually involved if this documentation was sought before college.

Test anxiety can be real, too! I had a student in Wyoming who **knew** all the answers to the test questions, but only when he was asked verbally by the professor out in the hallway. Staring at a test paper just made him freeze and his mind went blank.

It's hard to explain why the brain works the way it does, and people spend entire careers figuring that out! Yes, some students try to take advantage of these accommodations, just as some people take advantage of situations if they're impatient, unethical, lazy, or entitled.

But too many students don't get the help that would allow them to show their hard work, intelligence, and understanding of the material. They deserve that opportunity.

Sometimes, a student hasn't been diagnosed with a learning or processing disability yet, so they don't know they need the help. It won't always show up in grade school, and it hits hard when the workload is double at the college level. That student must get the diagnosis, or the college **cannot** provide services the student needs.

Again—it's the law. They want to help! And, once again, this is where the **student** must do the asking.

Yes, there are times when these issues are complicated enough that the student needs help communicating them to the office or needs help to even visit the office. That's not the same as the parent speaking for a child. Please remember the difference and the limitations of the staff at these offices!

Another underused office or group of employees can be found in the library on a college campus.

Some of us avoided the library as undergraduate students and paid the price. There are so many resources to help students with papers, presentations, and finding information. Some professors are now using a class day to take a field trip to the library. Oh, and they have books, lots of them! As well as movies, music, and, sometimes, even games to help with stress relief.

Some libraries have subject-specific tutors. Larger schools have offices dedicated to tutoring and what's known as Supplemental Instruction (SI). SI is mentioned elsewhere in this book, so I won't elaborate here. However,

I'll put in a plug that most SI offices can prove significant increases in a student's grades. And, almost always, that service is provided at no extra charge—as is everything a library offers. I won't say "free" because nothing at college is free! It's prepaid, by someone.

Bigger schools have many offices dedicated to students getting what Texas A&M called "the other education." There's so much a student can learn outside the classroom! That learning can take place in groups focused on:

- service,
- faith,
- sports,
- skills,
- charity,
- future careers,
- fraternities,
- dorms,
- hobbies,
- the military,
- leadership and more.

Texas A&M has more than 1,000 recognized student organizations. If a student has an idea or interest and couldn't find an organization, there's a straightforward process to create one (and someone to help do that).

Even small schools have student groups for leadership, volunteering, and chances to get experience. They're led by full-time professionals or advised by faculty who have volunteered to lead the group. All are valuable!

Some groups are competitive, while others welcome all. Most groups do recruit. At larger schools there's an advertised timeline, a set of requirements, and resources to help students navigate. All other things being equal, a student with a 3.5 GPA and other experiences on a résumé will have a better chance at a job than a student with only a 3.5 GPA.

Not all high school athletes or Junior ROTC leaders want to continue at the full-time level in college. But at bigger schools, there are still chances to compete or lead in such areas without being a Division 1 athlete or attending one of the service academies (i.e., the Army, Navy, Air Force, Marines, or Coast Guard).

Counseling on campus

Many campuses have counseling centers for students where full-time licensed counselors set appointments and handle emergency situations. Sometimes, they're psychiatrists or psychologists, but, most often, they're licensed counselors. They often have graduate degrees that prepare them to focus specifically on the needs of college students.

Many of these offices are overwhelmed with the needs and the numbers at their campus. Some schools train students to assist them with such services as Helpline call centers. My stepdaughter Karen Beloney Jenkins, who went on to get a master's degree in counseling, was part of that program.

I don't want to alarm you, but suicide attempts among college students are a huge issue. Many college professionals are trained to ask tough questions when they see a distressed student. If the answer indicates it, that professional (or student leader) knows where to get the best help. Not all campuses can support a full-time counseling center, but they can refer students to community resources.

Advisors and faculty

As I mentioned earlier, many campuses have a central advising center where any student can get help. Sometimes, within those centers are advisors who specialize in certain majors or divisions, even advisors who specialize in helping students who haven't yet figured out what to major in.

Beyond that advising center, there also are advisors among the faculty. Usually, those advisors are full-time faculty (teaching a full class load) who also have shown an interest in advising students. One school I worked at made sure every student was assigned to an advisor, and that name could be found online if they chose to look. That assigned advisor is only one resource for a student.

When I talked with parents, I made sure they understood that there were at least four professionals ready at any time to assist their students. Those four were:

1. assigned advisor,
2. a faculty member who teaches a class for that student,
3. the advisor within the student's major department, and
4. a staff member at the advising center or student affairs office

There also are professionals in a variety of roles around campus. Depending on the issue, their careers are devoted to helping those students. That's one reason it was so frustrating to hear a parent say their student told them that nobody on campus would help them.

I would encourage parents to say, at that point, "Who did you try to contact?" Also ask *how* they tried (e.g., email, in-person, phone, etc.). How *long* they waited for an answer. Was there anyone else who might be able to help? Instead, many would jump to the rescue and call someone higher "up the chain."

I had students say they dropped by my office, and I wasn't there, so, obviously, they couldn't count on me to help. If they happened to drop by between 1 and 2 p.m., my assigned lunch hour, then my door was locked, and the light was off. Yes, I was gone for that hour. I was there from 8 a.m. to 4:30 p.m. except for occasional trips to the copy machine or the bathroom. This is true for so many on-campus professionals.

Today's students seem to think that email is too slow and even text isn't fast enough! Most employees won't give out their cell numbers because they don't need to be getting texts at 2 a.m. Some do, though. But I'd strongly recommend using email, because it allows for a chain of record showing who said what to whom and when. Phone calls don't give you that trail of proof, which is so often needed.

I found it odd that so many students didn't even seem to know the name of their advisor, their professor, or anyone else they talk with. When we asked who told them something, we often got "That woman at the front desk." Or sometimes it's "Some guy in the main building."

I've had students not know how to contact a professor—even being in an in-person class. I'm certain that professors go over the syllabus at the start of every semester. And one of the things they're required to include is how to best contact them. It's almost always at the top of the first page, too. Sometimes, faculty choose email within the electronic part of a course.

Other times, they want students to use campus email. Some still prefer in-person appointments, and most have drop-in office hours. Some of the more "old school" instructors prefer phone conversations. Regardless, they have put their preference in writing, on the syllabus, available on day one of class—if not sooner.

I spent a lot of time explaining to students the typical "chain of command" on campus. If they're unhappy about something their instructor has done in class (or with grading, for example), they don't know what to do. I've spent time rehearsing a conversation with a student. I'd play the role of the professor, so they can get a little less nervous about the discussion.

I remind them that these instructors are experts in their subject. They deserve respect for earning academic credentials. But they're also people who go to Walmart, occasionally have a flat tire, and might even coach a kid's t-ball team. They're people, and most of them do love to teach and see students learn.

At some of the large research universities, there are some faculty who see teaching undergraduate classes as something they **must** do. They'd rather be doing their research or working with graduate students. At those same schools, some professors also are asked to teach classes with 300 students in them. That makes it tough to provide one-on-one service to each student.

I've also had professors tell me they wished more students would come to their office hours or make an appointment. At least send an email! And please send it before the last two weeks of class when it's panic time. It can be mathematically impossible to raise a grade by that point.

Some students did take the time and effort to meet with a professor, and, most of the time, they came back to me and told me how helpful it was! They got a whole new perspective on problem solving. It was even better when they took my advice and started building a working relationship with a professor at the beginning of the semester—*before* there was a problem. But some students came away from those meetings even more frustrated. That's when the chain of command became important.

In most schools, each faculty member has a department head (or department chair). That person takes the lead for a group of teachers in the same area (e.g., English literature). That's the next stop when working with a professor one-on-one doesn't go so well. That department chair will want to know what the student has already tried, and what result they got. It helps to have documented the conversation or the attempts at contact. Again, dropping by one time and finding an empty office isn't a true attempt at meeting.

If the student still isn't satisfied after meeting with a department chair, the next step is usually the dean. That individual is a little harder to meet with, if only because they have a lot of people wanting to get on their appointment calendar. Usually, an assistant sets up appointments, just to keep it all straight. Being kind to that assistant is a smart move!

Of course, the dean also reports to someone. That's usually a Vice President of Academic Affairs or someone with a similar title. That Vice President also reports to a President, who also reports to a Chancellor or a Board of Regents.

There are many names for all these positions, and there's a clear explanation of who reports to whom. It's almost always available on a school's website, so students know where to start and where to go next. Sometimes it's made even more clear which administrator handles which kinds of issues, especially at the larger schools.

Despite what angry parents often think, it does **not** make the most sense to leap to the vice president level as soon as something goes wrong. Often, miscommunication happens, or the student hasn't been paying attention to information provided earlier.

Too many parents are convinced their students would *never* do anything wrong, never miss a class, and always sit in the front row. Their students do *all* the required work. They contribute well-considered questions in every discussion. They put in days of studying in advance of every exam.

What a beautiful fantasy world that must be!

Yes, some students do all those things. Usually, though, those students don't run to mom or dad to solve issues for them.

Those students have started to learn how to ask for help, and where and when to ask. Those students are making full use of all the professionals on campus who want to help and have the right expertise to do so.

In my world as an advisor, those students made up for the others, the ones who were whining, who were looking for someone to blame, or who were trying to get points for showing up.

I used to think it was an attitude problem, but I've come to believe that it's because they were taught to do this, and it got results. It got their parents moving on their behalf. Why should they change that behavior if it keeps working?

One time, I made the mistake of asking whether these rescue-oriented parents were still going to keep doing this after college. What if their son got a full-time job and had a problem? Turns out, they do continue. As I mentioned earlier, I've talked to real-world professionals who had parents attend job interviews, demand a raise for their child, and protest a firing. This is *beyond* inappropriate. It's not allowing these young people to become functioning adults!

It may not be easy to shift from being a rescuer or enabler to a guide. But it's critical!

Whenever you can, as early as possible, start teaching your children to ask for help when they're the ones who need or want it.

Sure, you can be watching (from a distance) to make sure they're safe. But little-by-little, you need to remove yourself from the process as they get older.

You can rehearse the discussion with them. You can suggest a strategy. But I'd recommend making that suggestion only after asking them something like, "What do you think are some good ways to handle it?" You might be surprised with their strategy! And it gives them ownership of problem solving for themselves, which is a tremendous boost to their confidence.

It's so rewarding to get a phone call from your college kid to hear them say, "Mom! Guess what I took care of today!" Maybe you would have done it differently, and maybe they'll ask you for suggestions for how they could do it a little better the next time. But tread carefully in that area.

If you tell them how they **should** have done it, you've just knocked them down a few unnecessary pegs. Don't tell them unless they ask! This is a time for listening, feedback, and teaching. Not criticizing or ridicule. It's not easy to take this path, but it's what we're supposed to do as parents. We're supposed to raise adults who can then go on, perhaps, to raise more adults.

Allow your college student to learn how to find the right advisor for the situation. Step back and let them work with that someone to find a solution and to learn from the situation. Don't make it about you, or your brilliance in problem solving. Don't make it about whom you know in the president's office, and how much alumni clout you have.

Remember—there are always *at least* two sides to every story. Even if three of us were standing in the same room at the same time hearing the same discussion, we wouldn't all perceive it the same. We all have our filters of experience, bias, and perception. Somewhere in that mix will be what some call "truth." But the point here isn't truth. The point is finding a way to work through it all: the miscommunication, difficult situations, and uncomfortable issues. The even bigger point is learning, not just the subject matter in the classroom but also the ways of the world.

There will always be difficult people for your children to deal with (as you have experienced for yourself). Sometimes, that difficult person will be in authority over a situation. Sometimes, that difficult person is just doing his or her job. Sometimes that difficult person is the precious nephew of someone even more "important." That's the way our world works. The sooner your children are equipped to deal with it, the sooner they'll become positive contributors to our society.

Mentors

Mentors are one of the most overlooked resources for students. And they have a role that can be easily misunderstood.

Some campuses have students who are trained to be mentors for other students. I believe these are some of the most influential people on a college campus. Students tend to listen to other students—especially those who have what they want!

Sometimes, all a student wants are good grades. But other times, they see that those mentors have leadership roles, strong résumés, or a great job waiting for them after college. These mentors are so much closer in age to the students. It's nothing new to hear that peers are the strongest influences in most young people's lives. That's been around for ages!

Peer mentors aren't the only kinds that can help. Some campuses have community members who volunteer to mentor students. Maybe these mentors are the age of the parents, but they *aren't* the parents. That gives them a level of credibility right away that parents will never get.

Yes, there are students who have good relationships with their parents and seek their advice. Some seek it several times a day and won't make a move without mom's blessing. But in my view, that extreme isn't healthy. At what point do students start to rely on their own decisions? College is a good time—although sooner is better—to begin that "weaning." Peer mentors can often help with that transition.

My husband and I both served as academic mentors to a group of students in Texas A&M's Corps of Cadets. My husband was in that Corps back in the 1970s, so he had some understanding about what those students were going through. But his experience 40+ years ago isn't the same one they're going through. It has some common elements, and he gets points for "been there—done that," but today's world isn't the same on so many levels. The students did appreciate his perspective and often asked for his advice.

We were mentors to two different groups in the Corps. I would often refer my students to him, especially when it was a question about the Corps. And he would refer his to me if they needed help with navigating college, especially academics. He knew better, though, than to send anyone to me who needed help with math or science! I was the go-to for anything to do with writing, time management, or study skills in general.

That's part of what makes a mentor useful. Mentors know who else has answers. And the best mentors know when to say, "I don't know—and let me find someone who does." Referrals are a huge part of helping students! You want them to get the best possible answer from the most up-to-date and official source. You want to help stomp out their relying on "Yeah, but my friend said…"

Encourage your student to seek out a mentor on campus, and if there isn't a formal program for that, there are other ways to find a good one. Often, a mentor can be found among the leaders of organizations. Or professors can recommend students who have done well in the same academic area and are open to the idea of being a mentor. Or maybe you know someone who is a professional in the area your student is considering. Job shadowing is just one way to learn from that professional—perhaps a mentor-type relationship can be developed as well.

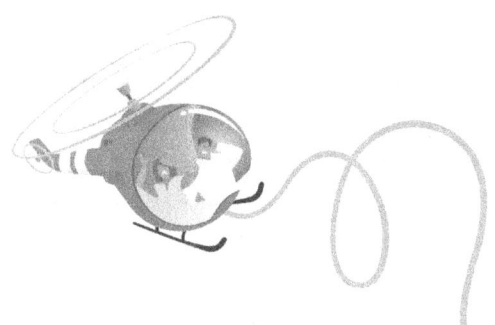

What's the parents' role?

I've spent a lot of time in this book telling you what I think parents shouldn't do. I'm a very positive person and like to focus on "yes" instead of "no." I'm a fan of saying "Remember!" instead of "Don't forget!" I was once told that kids remember the last word of what you yelled at them, so "forget" will be what sticks. I'm not sure whether that has any basis in research, but it did stick with me.

Maybe I've focused more on the "don't" side of this because I saw so much of it happening. That's part of what led me to write this book.

So, let's shift to what *should* be happening to successfully parent college-age kids.

I know that it's not always the parents doing the supporting. It can be older siblings, guardians, grandparents, foster parents, Godparents, and more. The two-parent home, made up of a father and a mother, isn't as common as it used to be. In my view, that's more than okay!

There are many ways to raise healthy kids into wonderful adults. The "traditional American" way may be the only way in the view of some people, but that's not true in my world.

Children who are parented with love, consistency, and healthy boundaries will flourish. None of us are in the position to say what the best parenting scenario is. I can tell you, for example, that I always felt like less of a "natural mom" with small children. I was better at the organizing, managing, planning, and running the household.

My first husband was a genius with small children. He didn't even mind smelly diapers! He could play on the floor with our kids for hours, making them his #1 priority (and they knew it). Luckily, we had agreed early on that we should each do the role that fit us best.

I sometimes think he got a shot that gave him instant mom abilities when our daughter was delivered by emergency C-section. I didn't get that shot. I was nervous, insecure, and terrified that I'd ruin the children with the slightest mistake. He was able to relax, make mistakes, learn from them, and just love the kids. How I envied him that ability! And how I was judged for our difference! I was able to step up a lot more when they got older, and, at that stage, he seemed a little unsure about his role.

I'm convinced that some of us—female or not—aren't a "natural" at parenting small children. I wish we could accept that and support people in the roles they're best at.

Sometimes, parents are trying to do it all alone. I don't know how that plays out without the parent completely being exhausted and burnt out! Anyone doing a good job as a parent will often be tired by it, even when they have a partner of some kind. So, I hope we can all be supportive of whatever design of a family seems to be healthiest for all involved. **And cut down on the judgment!**

Regardless of the person or persons taking the lead in the parent role, there are ways to do it well at the college level. What we're looking for here is **healthy** connections.

It's great that more of today's kids are in touch with their parents more often. I know my parents were thrilled (and shocked) to get a letter from me once a month when I was in college. Phone calls were even more rare, because this was a time before mobile phones. I saw them even less in person.

In 2019, I'm told that a large percentage of college students are in touch with one or more parent several times a day. I've been in meetings with students who couldn't (or wouldn't?) decide on which class to choose without calling mom first.

Many times, I had to diplomatically and assertively make sure the parent in the meeting knew the meeting was about the student—not about them. I'd speak to the student, looking them in the eyes instead of the parent.

If I could prevent a parent from joining us without offending someone, I would. I would make it clear that I would be focusing on the student, and the student could choose who is in the room as a supporter. Sometimes, it could get ugly, and sad. Some students gave up and let mom or dad run all over them—and try to run over me.

Being a parent myself, sometimes I was able to diffuse the situation. Other times, I wasn't so lucky.

What do healthy connections look like?

In my opinion, starting *before* college, parents should begin to step away and allow their children to start learning some life lessons. They should start allowing them to fail safely and learn from the failure.

Choosing classes isn't a life-or-death situation. Some parents take it on as if it were and have convinced their child they'll only make a mess of it without help.

How will that child learn to choose a job or a spouse? Don't we want them to be functioning adults sometime in their 20s (if not sooner)? We need to let go of our need to be the expert, to be *needed*, and, instead, be content to be consulted sometimes.

I mentioned before how delightful it's to be **asked** for help by my once-teenage and now-adult children. It wasn't easy to watch them mess things up. Sometimes, tears had to be dried. Sometimes they needed a good-sized Band-Aid. These are life lessons, and they must be learned. The more they learn this young (with less painful consequences), the smoother the transition to tougher decisions.

I can't tell you what a healthy connection looks like for you and your student. I can tell you it's probably less than what you think is necessary.

It's not cold-hearted to let the phone go to voice mail when you're at work. It's rarely a real emergency. Yes, there will be times when it **is** an emergency. Unless you're a trained medical professional, they should be dialing 9-1-1 instead of your number. That may sound harsh, but precious seconds are wasted by calling Mom or Dad instead of someone who can help in a true emergency.

We must teach our children what a real emergency is, and how to distinguish it from an inconvenience or frustration. Not only does that free up first responders to deal with real problems, it also frees you up to do whatever you spend your days doing. The bonus is this. It gives your children a chance to learn to solve something on their own (with appropriate help), then get the satisfaction of telling you how they did it. You then get to reinforce and coach. That's a much healthier role!

Before you say, "Here's what you should do!" consider saying, "What have you already tried?" Or, "Who have you already contacted about this?" Or the less subtle, "What did your advisor tell you?" or "What did the professor write in the syllabus?"

One of the many wonderful things my stepson and daughter-in-law have done is teach their kids how to order for themselves in restaurants. They also have the kids contact us (by phone or in person) to request sponsorship for a fund-raising project, which the parents know we will support. This is a training opportunity!

I remember taking my kids to my office and having them walk around and offer to show the Sally Foster wrapping paper catalog to my colleagues instead of **me** sending it around. I had asked ahead of time who was willing, but the kids had to make the actual sales pitch. That's one example of a way to start teaching them to ask for what they want or need and learn to hear "no" every now and then. It's a great opportunity to coach them on their approach, too.

Some children struggle with any kind of sales, so they want the help! But they don't need you to take it over. That just convinces them you think they're not capable, and it frees them from having to learn to do something most adults at some point have to do. I speak from experience here, having had to sell something as boring as the ads in a high school directory.

Find ways to teach your kids early on some of the skills they'll need later. For example, start teaching them cooking, cleaning, laundry, time management, effective communication, problem solving, and more. Let them try—and maybe fail. By college, it should be old hat.

They shouldn't need (or want) you to be in meetings with their advisor. They'll want you to go to the parent sessions of orientation instead of going with them to theirs—if they allow you to go at all!

I remember my parents dropping me off for my three-day orientation. It was longer because it included another try to raise my SAT scores. They told me when they'd return to pick me up. That was 1982, and I know things are different now, but somehow, I survived! Do I wish they'd stuck around? Nope. But my parents had both been to college and were familiar with the A&M campus already.

Was I a little insecure in my dorm room at age 17 that summer, not knowing anyone in my orientation sessions? You bet! Did I learn from that and get better by the time the Fall semester started? Yep! Did I meet a nice young man in the lobby of the dorm where I was studying and learn about Pepe Taco? Absolutely.

Figure out, with your children, what "healthy" connections look like. Figure out how you'll handle things when they have problems that they might be able to handle without you. Learn to move past the desire to be needed and move onto the delight of being wanted and consulted. It's much more satisfying, I assure you!

What's the student's role?

I'm still deciding how much to include in this chapter, because this book is about the parent (in my mind). I hate to think of parents handing this book to their student and saying, "Here—read this chapter on how to be a successful college student!"

That won't go well—even if you have a good relationship with your kids. It's even worse if they already roll their eyes when you try to talk about college, grades, or responsibility around the house.

Most people I know—even adults—don't react well to being told they need to read an article or book to make them better at something. There are diplomatic ways to approach that, but it's a minefield with teenagers.

See if you hear yourself saying this, "Hey, son! I'm reading a book on X topic, and I think you might get something out of it." See how fast they try to get out of that. They may even leave the room—rapidly.

Maybe you have an exceptional child or phenomenal relationship with them, and they say, "Thanks, Mom! I've been wondering how I can improve!" Sounds more like a sitcom to me, or sarcasm.

Typical teens don't want to be told how to improve themselves. It's hard enough to hear from teachers, coaches, and peers. Imagine, then, how eager they are to hear it from you. In my mid-50s, I still sometimes struggle to hear such things from my own loving, generous, helpful husband. Even when I've asked him to tell me whether I'm doing something wrong, and—if so—how to fix it.

Leaving pamphlets or books on their desk doesn't make it more likely they'll read it either. My parents tried that about some sensitive topics they weren't prepared to discuss (it was the '70s). My friends and I still laugh about that.

As I write this, I'm figuring out that I'm not going to get too specific. There are so many good books on student success in college! Read the Amazon reviews, make sure the date is at least within 4 years, and wait until your student asks (which they may never do) for help. They're already getting some of it from their high school guidance counselor and teachers. If they want more, it's readily available. The more you force it, the more they'll resist.

What these books will teach them should revolve around the following:
- Asking for help from the appropriate places
- Making sure to show up in class—every time
- Developing communication and conflict resolution skills
- Changing study skills to fit college-level material
- Getting rid of bad habits learned in high school
- Learning to design and follow a schedule—perhaps for the first time
- Safely using a new level of freedom in a new environment

It's much less important for them to learn how to:
- Get into the right fraternity
- Find out where the best parties are
- Choose the right gear for football tailgating.

They'll learn that—and much more—when they're on campus.

Much of it is specific to the school they choose to attend. So, these books written at a national level of general information may not be all that useful anyway. Orientation at most schools is thorough and often overwhelming.

The scariest thing to me when I was in the "dorm mom" role was all the misinformation they would get from peers. Of course, they trusted that more than they trusted the old fogies at the front making a presentation.

You can't change that behavior among their age group. Peers will always be their preferred source—until they learn from that mistake. It seemed to me that my job was trying to ensure they did that learning without injury or destruction of property. I wasn't always able to pull that off.

Just know that there are plenty of truly high-quality resources out there for your student. Your suggesting them will not make them more attractive (in most cases). It's somewhat scary and usually disappointing to realize this, but it's what I've seen over and over.

You're a blessed parent if your 17-year-old comes to you and asks you to buy a book about college success. You've either done something truly exceptional raising that child or you've got an exceptional child. That's exactly the kind of college student I'd love to coach, but that's also not the norm. If they want to hire me, I'm up for it! My email is in the introduction.

Most of us choose to either raise our kids the opposite way from how our parents did or a lot like the way we were raised. No, it's not an absolute. It's on a continuum. And often, we learn in our later years as parents that some of what we hated in our upbringing was quite wise.

About other things, we wonder what on earth they were thinking! There are no right answers to this—just loving attempts.

What if not college?

Maybe you got to this point in the book and are convinced your child isn't going to college. Maybe they're not ready. Maybe it's not affordable right now. Maybe their grades aren't what they need to be. Maybe they simply don't want to. As I've said, there are plenty of reasons why your child may not be headed to college. Most of them are valid. Forcing a student into school when they aren't ready/willing/able is a bad idea. I can't put it much better.

College might not be a fit based on career goal, learning style, or timing, in addition to the reasons I mentioned above. Even if it's affordable and they can get in, it may not be the right time.

My daughter and I have a friend from Wyoming, Alix, whose husband Jacob chose to move from his hometown in Texas to attend WyoTech in Laramie, WY. He completed their core diesel technology course and then the advanced diesel specialty program. His parents both have four-year degrees from universities, but he felt that the traditional classroom setting of a university wasn't a good fit for him. He did attend a traditional college for a year before transitioning to WyoTech. He figured out that completing all the basic/core courses for a traditional four-year degree wasn't the best use of his time.

Alix says Jacob was fortunate to have two parents who were very understanding and helped him navigate all the different options he had available to him, instead of pushing him too hard in one direction.

If they're not going for the right reasons—**their** reasons—they're starting out at a huge disadvantage. They're taking up class space and using someone's money to do something they don't want to do or aren't prepared to do.

The number of students taking remedial classes in reading, writing, and math is rising at a staggering rate.

Of course, we couldn't call it "remedial," because that could make people feel bad about themselves. The harsh truth is, if they can't read and write at a college level, they'll struggle terribly. And that's at the community college level, where instructors want the students to succeed. They don't have to "weed out" any students like they do at some universities where space is limited in upper-level classes.

I don't blame the high schools for sending students to college who are unable to perform at college level. Often, those schools and teachers are forced to focus on standardized tests and passing rates. They don't have the time or personnel to approach each student in the way that works best for each student's learning style. And they're pressured to pass some on to the next level in too many cases. What a lousy state of affairs for our educational system in the United States! I hope someone can solve it soon.

Meanwhile, there are barely enough slots at community colleges in the "developmental" classes. Many universities won't even admit students who don't have the right scores and grades. The ones who do admit them have some sort of "bridge" program to help students get stronger in basic skills. They'll tell you that a semester of "make up" work will delay graduation at least a semester.

Graduation myths

That brings me to a quick side note. You may have heard the phrase graduating "on time." Back in my day, that meant four years, or eight semesters, at a college or university. It meant at least 120 credits by the end of a bachelor's degree. Taken at the rate of about 15 credits per semester (without attending in the summer). Those who failed courses or changed their major more than once were often around on a more drawn-out plan. Some joked about being on the "Decade Plan" or taking "Victory laps" instead of graduating as a first-time senior.

The reality is that many of the more difficult programs, such as engineering of any kind, can't be completed in 120 hours anymore. And many students struggle with some of the core classes, such as calculus.

My father, back in the 1940s, had to take organic chemistry three times before he mastered it. My husband is one of few people I know who passed thermodynamics on the first try, but he needed five tries at differential equations (popularly known as DiffEQ). I don't even know what you **do** in that kind of class, so I would probably have failed it forever. I'm just not wired for that kind of thinking, and I've learned to be okay with that!

Realize that graduating in four years—freshman, sophomore, junior, and senior—isn't the norm anymore, especially without summer classes. I heard a percentage once, from a respectable source, of how many students do that. It was below 25%. There's more recent research on this, and a lot depends on the major and the school. There are many reasons why this is the case, and I don't know them all.

I want you to know that it's no longer the expectation for the average student, just like it's no longer the norm for an adult to work for one company for 30 years and get a gold watch at retirement. The loyalty isn't there in either direction. It's one of many ways our society has changed, and the students don't need the added pressure of being told to "finish on time."

For some students, college isn't the right thing *right now*. It will be later, perhaps. There are many ways to get them through this time when it's not right and help them figure out for themselves when and if it's right for them.

Depending on why it's not the right time, the path to college later can vary. Yes, if they delay, it could be a lot harder to interrupt work (or whatever they're doing) and go back to class. Fewer scholarships could be available, so it could cost more. They could have to deal with a work schedule, children, or feeling out of place among the 18-year-olds. Those are realities, but they don't need to prevent students from going back to school later. It's *not* always true, as some people say, that if you don't go right away, you'll never go. In fact, I've seen that it's getting even less true in recent years.

If a student starts college when they're not ready, it can quickly become obvious that it won't work. It's easy to overlook that feeling or deny the reality. But when grades come in, there's no avoiding it. Scholarships can be lost based on low grades or reduced credit hours. For this reason, among many others, it can be better to wait.

That's a great discussion to have **before** the family is all sitting around at Thanksgiving and questions come up about how well college is going. It would be nice if fewer family gatherings included humiliating discussions. You know, the ones about grades, engagements, or weight loss. Not likely, but I can dream.

For the umpteenth time, I'm going to mention that the decision to attend, or not, and when, must belong to the **student**! The **student** must do the work, go to class, and stick it out when things get rough. They must want it more than you want it for them!

Now that I've repeated that, I want to share an email sent to me recently by one of my favorite students from Vol State. I hesitated to include it verbatim, because she gives me *way too much* credit for her success (and calls me Professor Adair—which I haven't earned). But she asked that I quote her, because it's such an important experience for her to share. Just so you know, this student sometimes brought her mom with her, and her mom played exactly the role I hoped she would.

"Hello Professor Adair!

I am so happy to be emailing you without some crazy questions about credit hours or if I should switch my major again! ;) I am so glad you thought of me as one of the students who should contribute to your book. If anyone should write a book on keeping young people and their parents sane through college, it is you.

When I came to you a few years ago, I had been going to the same advisor since I graduated high school. In the beginning, I was just glad to have someone to sit down and talk with. However, as time went on, this wasn't enough. He would say things like, "That's really up to you," and, "If you think so!" This was my first time in college, and prior to this I had only made class suggestions on a slip of paper before each semester of high school. I knew absolutely nothing about the college website, scheduling, or credit hours. They did not prepare us for that in high school. I found myself trying to choose overlapping classes and even trying to select a class that was given on a different campus! Needless to say, his, "It's up to you!" attitude was no help to me. I was lost, confused, and finally, in between a rock and a hard place. Not ONCE was I referred to an online class option. He never told me that I could switch my major if necessary.

As my career in music began to take off with an offer of two two-week tours in both Chile and the UK, I remember sitting at the table with my understanding mom and my boyfriend of four years. The first thing I remember saying was, "Guys... I don't want to disappoint you, but..."

We discussed what I was thinking. But I find it funny now that I didn't once think about disappointing myself or harming MY future.

My mom and my boyfriend both reminded me that they wouldn't be disappointed in me at all, but that I probably would be in myself in the long run. When I found out about the TN Promise in 2015, I had not once thought about going to college. I honestly had no interest and just wanted to go straight to music, debt free. When I learned that for eight hours of community service a semester, I could have two free years of college, I challenged myself. I mean... Hey! It's free right?

At first, I took the chance because it wasn't going to cost me anything but gas money. However, after the first semester, it became so much more. It became a personal challenge.

"Wow... I'm NOT dumb. This ISN'T impossible. I WANT to finish."

But as I mentioned before, I was now trapped between my passion and my determination. I went in for one final meeting with my previous advisor to tell him that I was going to quit, and if I remember correctly, he wasn't there that day. Little did I know, this was God's way of pushing me towards someone else!

I was then sent to "another advisor."

I sat down and immediately felt that I was being given more attention than I'd received in the past two years of school. I admitted why I came to school for a meeting that day, and Professor Adair responded with, "Ok, so here are some options!"

Words that would keep me in school.

In this short meeting, I was given amazing options.

I don't believe any young person is a natural born quitter. I think they just work with what they have, and at this point, I had no realistic options. I didn't want to quit. I felt I had to, until this meeting in which I was told that I could switch my major. I NEVER would've thought of that on my own, and my previous advisor would've never suggested it. I was also told that this new major would accommodate online classes, allowing me to travel. I cannot tell you what a weight this was off my shoulders. She asked me something that no other educator had ever asked me or cared about: "Where are you getting the most experience for the things that you want to do in the future? The classroom, or on the road/stage?"

So many educators only push in-class education. I never even thought about studying something else college wise and getting my musical training outside of school. I had been taking some music classes in school but didn't plan on being a music teacher. So, my honest answer was that my best learning moments were happening on the road, doing what I planned on doing for my entire life. We then tailored my classes around this understanding.

I stayed in school, and last December I graduated with my associate degree.

But my persevering didn't just come from that one meeting. It came from hands on guidance from an amazing educator who I KNEW cared about my future as well as my college experience.

She answered my emails in DETAIL (so important to me) and continued to meet with me when I needed help. She didn't hold my hand through the process, she taught me. I honestly feel that when I have college-age kids, I'll be more helpful to them because I had someone to watch when I was in their shoes.

I feel that everything Professor Adair did contributed to keeping me in school. Not only her amazing options, but her optimism. I could tell that she cared if I finished or not.

I have never felt so accomplished as the day I walked across the stage at Vol State. While I did have some amazing teachers along the way, no one was as important to me as Professor Adair. I proved something to myself and to my family and friends that day. I went from someone with no plans of college, to someone who didn't want to give up on college, to someone who conquered college.

A good educator means everything to the student. We've never done this before and come to college so nervous and truly unprepared. While it is beneficial to the student to do things for themselves, they cannot figure out everything BY themselves. It would be like telling someone to go fix the brakes on a car. If they were never taught how to, how could they be expected to succeed?

Thank you for everything. I'm sorry this was so lengthy, but I can't say enough to describe how grateful I am for you coming into my life! Your approach works. You didn't scare me; you gave me hope. Please spread what you did with parents and educators alike! If we had more people like you, I know graduation rates would skyrocket!"

This student may be exceptional in her needs and her approach. But she isn't completely unique in that. Not everyone already knows what they want to do as an adult and is already doing it. Sometimes, they are and don't even realize it. Sometimes, they'll need more credentials to keep doing it and making a living at it. Some just want to prove to themselves that they can do it—especially if anyone told them they couldn't.

Online classes

This student's situation may not be typical. But it highlights the fact that there are options other than college. Or—if college is still something that matters to them—other ways to attend. That's part of the beauty of the technology we have now. I know in the "old days" they had correspondence courses, but this is much more rapid. It can also be tricky.

Some students think it'll be "easier" to take online classes. Those students are often disappointed if that style of learning doesn't fit for them or if they're uncomfortable with technology. If they're not good about planning and initiative, then they'll quickly learn that these classes are much more difficult.

Attendance is a whole new idea in these classes. Deadlines are different. Support is different. The interaction is different. Some classes, just by the nature of their content (e.g., biology), are more difficult on a computer. Some students just do better with the in-person interaction.

I'm one of those people! I learn more from in-person discussion, questions, interaction, and the need to show up and be seen in person. Especially in math-based classes. The harder the subject, the more I want to be in the room with the person trying to teach it to me. Many people discover that when they try an online class. For some, though, it's the only option that their life and schedule will allow (as was the case with the student who wrote that message to me).

Not now, but maybe later

If, even with the flexibility of modern learning methods, college is still not the right fit or the right fit **now**, there are other workable options. I'll list just a few here in broad categories because I know of people who pursued them successfully. Many came back to go to school—more prepared and more eager. Others figured out they didn't want or need college to have a successful life—by their own definition (which remains the most important one). Your student can consider:

- Trade school (instead of traditional college), including technical colleges and specific training programs
- Working in a job to earn money, or to see if it's what they want to do
- Taking a "gap year," something people in the United States are starting to investigate the way Europeans have for a long time
- Service, including military, Peace Corps, or other types of service to society.

All these are useful ways to spend time and money. Especially if, during that time, the student grows up enough to figure out what they want to do next with their life. And please remember the emphasis is on **next**—not **forever**.

Some people out there, called "Scanners" by author Barbara Sher, have several things they want to do. They may have struggled with the way society used to want us all to pick one thing and stick with it forever. Once they learn that's not necessary, and that there are many ways to fulfill more than one passion or interest, they're much happier.

Here's where I wholeheartedly recommend Barbara's books *Wishcraft* and *Refuse to Choose*. The first one was written decades ago and helped me figure out my career path. What a gift it was to me then, and still is now. The other book is more recent and has been embraced by Scanners all over the world. It could be that your child fits this category and could find great relief in the idea of not having to choose one thing forever.

As I mentioned in an earlier chapter, few people **really** know what they want to do with their lives when they're first asked. Sure, we answer "astronaut" or "fire fighter" or "baseball player" when we're young.

At that point, almost nobody knows exactly what it takes to successfully do those things for a living. The work, the education, the years! They just know it appeals to them for some reason.

It could be that they have no aptitude for that "dream job." People who get motion sickness will struggle to be jet pilots, much less astronauts. People with horrible hand-eye coordination will have extra challenges in some sports. It's not that they're not "good enough" to try that career. It just might not be a fit.

That's okay!

We can't all be doctors, lawyers, engineers, movie stars, or Super Bowl MVP. Sometimes, it's a matter of ability. Other times, it's a discovery that what it looks like on a day-to-day basis isn't at all appealing. What we see in the media about some jobs is far from realistic. That's something many people don't figure out until they've spent years thinking they're going to do that job. They've said it so often they feel like they'll look foolish if they don't pursue it.

To me, it's much worse to be miserable in a job than it is to say, "Wow—did I ever have limited information when I made that choice!" We should be able to change our minds when we get more relevant facts. And when we see how our skills and preferences interact with the career's requirements. Why is that not the norm yet?

There are many ways for students to get a better idea of what different jobs require. But again—the students must be in a place mentally and emotionally where they can truly take it in. It must be **their** idea to explore it. Sometimes, that doesn't become clear until they've taken their first biology class and realized science is the last thing they want to do. Sometimes, it happens when they do a week of job shadowing and realize the "nitty gritty" of a job is most of that job, and it isn't something they want to do.

If it happens soon enough, they realize choosing the wrong major can be prevented. Or they can change it. The student can choose to do assessments to help make the best "next choice" more obvious.

I'm not a licensed career counselor, but I'm certified in at least three systems that help students with these choices. There are more!

The ones I've been trained in are:

- the Myers-Briggs Type Inventory (MBTI), which is often mistakenly called a "personality test,"
- the Strong Interest Inventory (SII), and
- the StrengthsFinder method, now known as Clifton Strengths by Gallup.

These are incredibly useful assessments—**not tests.** They give results based on the individual's input about such things as preferences, interests, and natural tendencies. They do **not** tell someone what they should do for a living. They do provide invaluable information about what should be a great fit!

I've had many students do a professional consultation after the assessments—which is how it should be done. They walk away knowing new things about themselves, having a new vocabulary to discuss it with the most helpful people, learning about possibilities that never occurred to them before. Some high school counselors can provide access to these assessments, or information on how to get them at low (or no) cost.

That's the kind of information they need to start with. Then they should be reassured that the choice isn't written in blood or stone. It's what's *next*, for *them*, based on what they know *right now*. That eases the pressure, and again, makes it about them. See a theme here?

College isn't for everyone, and definitely not right after high school for many people. That doesn't mean those individuals are less intelligent, underachievers, or losers. People who stop going aren't always "dropouts." Those are labels and judgments made by people with limited information, and something going on in their own world that makes them feel the need to disparage someone else's decisions.

Getting an education, in some form or fashion, is a wonderful thing! I've devoted most of my adult life to being part of that process. There are few things more satisfying to me than leading someone through the process of finding the right fit for them, right now. It's like unlocking a secret set of rooms for them. Letting them decide which one(s) to walk through. Then being able to reassure them that I'll be here when they need help—or someone else who cares will take my place. What can be more fun than that?

In fact, let me close by sharing with you the three quotes I've had as part of my email signature for years. Maybe this will explain why I was so passionate as I wrote this book. I hope it's been helpful to you, and I'd be honored to hear if there are ways I can help. Thank you for reading, and please email me at Becky@Not13thGrade.com if you have questions, comments, or want to work with me as a coach or as a presenter.

"To love what you do and feel that it matters…how could anything be more fun?" Katharine Graham, American publisher

"It is our choices that show what we truly are, far more than our abilities." Professor Albus Dumbledore (from the Harry Potter series)

"When I stand before God at the end of my life, I would hope that I would have not a single bit of talent left and could say: 'I used everything you gave me.'" Erma Bombeck, humorist

Rebecca's Recommended Resources

The books listed below must, by nature, be somewhat general. They don't claim to apply to every school. The better ones recommend you contact the actual school in question to get the most accurate, up-to-date information. Here are my favorites (alphabetically by title):
- *A Starter Guide to College for Clueless Students & Parents*, by Seeker
- *Dear Parents: A Field Guide for College Preparation*, by McGee and Farrell
- *Flying Without a Helicopter: How to Prepare Young People for Work and Life*, by Connell
- *Gap Year: How Delaying College Changes People in Ways the World Needs*, by O'Shea
- *Getting to Calm: Cool-Headed Strategies for Parenting Tweens + Teens*, by Kastner
- *Give Them Wings: Preparing for the Time Your Teen Leaves Home*, by Kuykendall & Gilbert
- *I'd Listen to My Parents If They'd Just Shut Up*, by Wolf

- *Letting Go, Sixth Edition: A Parent's Guide to Understanding the College Years,* by Coburn and Trekker
- *Out to Sea: A Parents' Survival Guide to the Freshman Voyage,* by Radi
- *Parenting the New Teen in the Age of Anxiety: A Complete Guide to Your Child's Stressed, Depressed, Expanded, Amazing Adolescence,* by Duffy
- *That Crumpled Paper Was Due Last Week,* by Homayoun
- *You're on Your Own (But I'm Here if You Need Me): Mentoring Your Child During the College Years,* by Savage
- *Your Freshman Is Off to College: A Month-by-Month Guide to the First Year,* by Hazard and Carter

One final note about these resources. Any book, website, or group that claims to have all the answers or be able to condense this whole issue into "5 easy steps" is something to view cautiously.

This isn't an easy issue, no matter how good your parenting skills or how smart your student. It's just like when you were expecting your first child. You found yourself terrified after reading *What to Expect When You're Expecting* because they included *all possible disasters*. So, be careful about what and how much you read. Too much information can be confusing, contradictory, and overwhelming.

The idea is to help calm your fears, prepare you to guide your student, and make the best use of the right resources for your own situation. Nobody else can make your decisions for you!

Acknowledgements

Countless friends and colleagues have been supportive during my book creation adventure, and some were able to actually read through the rough draft and provide helpful comments. I truly appreciate the time that it took and the thought that went into their suggestions. Others offered their stories and experiences to help make this book more useful to the reader. Without these contributions, this book would still be just an idea. My gratitude goes out to Kathy L. Harris, Debbie Nanz Bush, Heather Welch Tottingham, Sue Foster, Thea Danos, Suzi Nazimek, Ginger Thompson Fish, Jill Notdurft Waldrop, and Chuck Beloney.

It's hard to describe the kind of expert support I received from my coach, Sloane Ketcham, and the self-publishing pros in the SPS Mastermind community. They've been willing to share their mistakes, lessons, and tips so quickly and freely. What a difference it made! I also appreciate the skills of my editor, Wayne Purdin, who reinforced what I already knew—that you can't trust yourself to be the final editor of your own work!

While they are also mentioned in the dedication, I must further acknowledge the trust shown to me by the first readers of this book—my own kids. They each have a chapter focused on them, and it's *personal*. Before anyone else was given a look at the rough draft, I asked for their blessing. Both willingly gave it, along with incredibly valuable suggestions. Thank you, Chelsea and Davis, for letting me use your stories.

About the author

Rebecca (Becky) Adair has been writing most of her life—but this is the first time she's published a book! After 30 years working at colleges and universities, Becky created a "patchwork of possibilities" chart so she can choose how to spend her days. This ability to choose is just further proof to her that there's a God and that He loves her!

Becky has two children from a previous marriage and two stepchildren from her current marriage. Two of the children live less than five miles away. The stepchildren provided the delight of grandchildren, long before Becky felt old enough to be a grandmother.

Becky is known for being super-organized and talking with her hands. She collects coloring books (and the colors to use in them), board games, puzzles, and non-fiction books. The fiction she reads—as a reward for getting something important finished—is donated when she's done.

When weather allows, Becky shoots archery in her backyard, wishes she could play more tennis and ping-pong, and sits on the back patio admiring middle Tennessee. She rates sunsets while drinking wine with her husband. Becky also plays the organ when nobody is listening and sings along with all the songs she knows. She loves getting to travel more, especially with friends and family (and friends who *are* family) while trying not to get so emotionally involved in Aggie sports.

She is eager to write her next book, so stay tuned!

Can You Help?

Thank you for reading my book!

I really appreciate all feedback, and I love hearing what you have to say.

Plus, I need your input to make the next version of this book and my future books better.

Please leave me an *honest* and *constructive* review letting me know what you thought of the book.

Thanks so much!

—Becky Adair

www.ingramcontent.com/pod-product-compliance
Lightning Source LLC
Chambersburg PA
CBHW071202070526
44584CB00019B/2892